AMAZING GRAYSON

AMAZING GRAYSON

Jerry Broadway

Broadway Bound Press – St. Louis, Missouri

These are my memories, from my perspective, and I have tried to represent events as faithfully as possible. I have changed some names to protect individuals' privacy.

To request permissions, contact the author at jerrybway@gmail.com. Author's agent says no one ever reads this page. If you made it this far, send an email to the author so he can rub it in said agent's face.

ISBN **9798673640807**

First paperback edition August 2020

Edited by: Jessica Keet

Cover art by: Daphne Broadway/Jerry Broadway
Layout by : Daphne Broadway/Lori Kehoe
Photographs by: Daphne Broadway

For Mom, Dad, and Mamaw Clark

On behalf of Grayson, this book is dedicated to Nonnie Harrison, aka *Nee-Nee*, a great Mother, a wonderful Mother-In-Law, and Grayson's favorite person in the world. We know that because he steals our phones and calls her around forty-two times a day...

Table of Contents

PROLOGUE...1

THE BALLAD OF BLIND MELON CHITLIN'...1

THE STUPID LEADING THE BLIND..............20

WHEN JERRY MET DAPHNE 26

CALLING DR. LOVE.......................................32

ONE ROLL OVER THE LINE 43

CHAPTER 6 52

THE ALMOST NOT-SO-HAPPY ENDING........52

TIME TO PUT A RING ON IT 56

NOT EXACTLY CHARLES AND DI 66

THAT ESCALATED QUICKLY!..........................72

THE QUEEN AND THE PRINCESS 79

MOVIN' ON UP – PART 1.................................86

OH, RIGHTY, WE HARDLY KNEW YE 92

AN AWESOME GOD 102

CHANDLER, OLD JOE, AND GEORGE........106

MOTHER'S INTUITION...................................112

A CONVERSATION WITH GOD 118

PLAN THE WORK...124

WORK THE PLAN...127

THE DEVIL IN THE FRONT OFFICE 135

WHEN IT ALL GOES SOUTH.......................145

PORTRAIT OF A MIDLIFE CRISIS 151

DO'S AND DON'TS 183

DOCTORS ARE NOT IN CHARGE 188

THE BEST WORST CHRISTMAS EVER 196

MOVIN' ON UP – PART 2 205

A STAR IS BORN 208

MOVIN' ON UP – PART 3 213

LIFE WITH THE G-MAN 219

OH, THE PLACES YOU'LL GO! 226

EPILOGUE 230

Foreword

When you think Jerry Broadway, co-host of the Bud and Broadway Show (spell out the word "and"), you probably think of the philosophical half of the team with the dry wit and a great laugh who usually remains in the "safe zone". Or maybe you consider him the more grounded of the two. The family man with the special needs kid. If that's the Broadway who comes to mind, then your perception is spot on. But wait....there's more!

Beyond the microphone and notoriety is the Jerry Broadway I know. The one who made a big, messy splash into my life over thirty years ago when he caught the attention of my little sister, Daphne. He was the full-on Redneck Trashy guy, minus the Skoal can ring in his back pocket and the wife beater t-shirt. The guy I now not only call my brother, but my friend.

When she introduced him, I immediately noticed his curly mullet that needed some serious styling. The next thing that caught my attention was the smell of cheap cologne. You know, the kind that lingers in a room or on your clothes when you hug a little old lady at church, but for men. He wore acid washed, no-named jeans and a pair of off-branded white tennis shoes that probably came from Wal-Mart. But I also noticed that he was kind of cute and he was a pretty nice guy.

However, I knew he would not be well received by our family no matter how great his personality was.

As with most teenagers and young adults, Daph wasn't giving up. She was determined to make everyone love her new beau as much as she was starting to. It only took me looking at the happiness in her eyes to jump on the Broadway bandwagon because as long as my little sister was happy, so was I. So it was up to me to help fix it. During that process, I grew very fond of this goofy redneck. To the point that I was all in on Team Jerry. And it didn't take long before I too began falling in love with him.

Over the years I have not only loved Jerry, but I've admired and appreciated him. He has proven himself on so many levels, even when he made bad choices. Through the years he and my sister have fallen on some very hard times, but he has never questioned God's plan for his life. He may have plugged his ears for a minute because he didn't like the plan, but haven't we all? You'll read some things in this book about him that will shock you and maybe even disappoint you, but don't be so quick to judge. If I am still his biggest fan, then I promise he's worthy of your mercy.

Through his love of not only his children, but all children, he has led campaigns throughout his career for numerous agencies who serve them, like the Salvation Army Angel Tree Program. He launched the radio leg of this program in 1995 in Dothan, Alabama and carried it to Jackson, Mississippi in 1999. Over a ten-year span, he and his radio partners were able to provide Christmas gifts to over 11,000 kids. This accomplishment has him listed in the Salvation Army's

1999 Decade of Heroes book for Alabama. Then, a few years ago, the Shriner's Children's Hospital in St. Louis, Missouri lost all their Christmas toys to a fire. Without blinking an eye, Jerry and Bud led their audience to replace all those Christmas toys and continued that program for several years. I could go on and on about how he has raised awareness and funds for organizations like The Red Cross, Folds of Honor, and The American Cancer Society, but the one campaign that made me the proudest of him was when he used his celebrity status to raise awareness for victims of child abuse. In 1998, he launched "Jerry's Rooftop Campout for Kids" where he camped out on the roof of the local Walmart for 3 days and raised almost $100,000 for local agencies! This effort earned him the title of South Alabama's Public Citizen of the Year for 1998. He would never mention this honor, but I will never stop mentioning it.

My admiration of Jerry is multi-faceted, but the two areas he excels in is being a daddy and a husband. I know there are some great dads out there, but I have witnessed very few who have made the impact that Jerry has made. And as far as husbands go, he's one to be admired. As a matter of fact, for years I longed to find my own "Jerry" (and I finally did). Jerry will do whatever it takes to make sure his family is taken care of. I've seen him work three jobs just to make sure his family had everything they needed and my sister could continue to be at home to take care of their children.

I could write an entire book on the Jerry I know, but I am not the wordsmith he is, so I'll let him speak for himself. Just know that you are getting the part of Jerry

Broadway that he doesn't share freely. He has removed all his inhibitions to provide you with this very entertaining autobiography that will hopefully bring you laughter as well as tears through his well-written words.

Stephanie Walters
Sister-in-Law, paying Facebook super-fan, critic, proofreader, sounding board, and advisor. (when going up against my sister)

PROLOGUE

I *don't know. I've only seen this once in my career.* Eleven words. Eleven bullets coated in a cloak of despair, dipped in fear, kissed by Satan, and fired from a weapon forged in hell. Our pediatrician, Dr. Robert Benak, was on the phone when he fired those projectiles straight through my soul. Moments before, my wife and I were anxiously optimistic as we waited for this call. We had been waiting for two days for the results of the test, and today would be the day we got answers. The test in question was an MRI of the brain of our six-month-old son, Grayson, and those answers we were so optimistic about would soon leave us sitting on the edge of our bed, broken and weeping.

We had known something wasn't right with Grayson for several months. He was six months old, but he was still the same baby he was the day we brought him home from the hospital. There was no rolling over, very few sounds, no measurable development of any kind. Then the eye thing started. I called it *the eye thing* because my knowledge of the human eye and its inner workings at that stage of my life would have fit on the head of a pin.

It started slowly, his eyes randomly pulling to the middle, and then drifting back to their original position. Then the twitching came. His pupils began moving left-to-right in a jerking motion. The longer each episode lasted, the faster they would gyrate. The speed would reach such a level that if you were looking at his pupils during one of these episodes, they would look blurry. I could not imagine what it was like to be on the other side of those eyes. It had to be maddening. All I could think of was the poor little guy trying to focus on something with his eyes moving uncontrollably. We had to do something.

Our first stop was to the office of Dr. Benak, a man who had earned my respect when Grayson was only a few weeks old and spiked a fever. Back then we were terrified, and when we arrived at the ER, they told us our regular pediatrician was not available or on call that weekend, but Dr. Benak was on duty for pediatric patients. The resident who was treating Grayson wanted to do a spinal tap. I refused to allow it until we spoke to a pediatrician. A few minutes later, a tall, slender man who looked just like James Taylor entered our lives. He gave Grayson a quick once-over, checked his chart, and promptly agreed with the original diagnosis that a spinal tap was needed to rule out meningitis.

When I balked a second time at the thought of that insanely long needle being inserted into the back of my child, James Taylor got all up in my grill. *Mr. Broadway*, he said, in a tone more reminiscent of the last verse of *Steamroller Blues* than the calming refrain of *Sweet Baby James, if you don't allow me to do this, and it's meningitis, he may not survive.* I could tell by his tone and the look in his eyes that he wasn't messing around. I stepped aside and let him do his work. Incidentally, Grayson did NOT have meningitis, just a nasty inner ear infection. We found that out after several days in the hospital awaiting test results when Grayson's regular pediatrician stopped by for a final check before discharging us. He said everything looked great, and as he left I said, *what about his ears? Dr. Benak said they looked infected.* He looked at me as if I had a third eye, flipped a few pages in Gryason's chart and said, *Oh yeah, he does have an ear infection. Let's keep him on the antibiotics for a few more days.* Daphne and I looked at each when he left the room, gave a sigh of relief and a prayer of thanks, and immediately decided that Dr. Benak was going to be Grayson's new doctor.

After checking out Grayson's eyes, Dr. Benak recommended we see a specialist. His referral to that specialist was the first step in a journey that continues to this day, seventeen years later.

The pediatric ophthalmologist we visited taught us a new word. The word was *nystagmus*. That is the official medical term for *the eye thing*. After putting Grayson through a battery of tests, her determination was, to be honest, a bit vague. The crazy movement of the eyes was, indeed, nystagmus. The cause of the nystagmus was unclear. She explained that it could be physiological, neurological, or worse, caused by a tumor on the front of his brain pressing against the optic nerve.

Once she dropped that bomb in our lap, she went on to say that lots of babies have nystagmus, and simply grow out of it. Another test was needed to determine which scenario best fit Grayson. She wanted to rule out the tumor before we moved on, and we supported that idea wholeheartedly. The test she ordered was the MRI that would change the course of our lives forever.

When Daphne, Grayson's mom, and the love of my life, answered the phone, she immediately handed it to me when she heard Dr. Benak's voice. Optimism quickly turns to blind panic when you get this sort of call about one of your kids. If someone had been there for me to pass the phone to, there is a good chance I would have. It's such a strange mix of emotions when you're the parent of a child with an unknown medical issue, wanting to know everything while not wanting to know a damned thing.

I took a deep breath, put him on speaker, and listened to the results. They were unfathomable. In his calm, caring, fatherly delivery, Dr. B began teaching me more new words. He diagnosed Grayson with two conditions. The main one was Agenesis of the Corpus Callosum. The second had an even more ridiculous name: Hypoplasia of the Vermis of the Cerebellum.

I don't know how many times he had to explain it to me. I stood there in our bedroom, phone in my hand, looking Daphne in the eyes as James Taylor delivered the news. After the initial blow of what he was saying, all I heard was the dull, monotone *wah wah wah* of Charlie Brown's teacher speaking to one of the Peanuts gang on the phone. When that sound faded, and the pounding of my heart subsided in my ears, I finally garnered enough knowledge to become paralyzed with fear and started in with the questions.

The good news from the test was the lack of a tumor on the optic nerve. That part of the report was fantastic. Unfortunately, while looking at the MRI, Dr. B noticed something was...missing. Grayson's brain was not whole. He had been born with not one, but two, neurological brain defects. The Corpus Callosum, a network of fibers that carries messages from one hemisphere of the brain to the other, was missing. The Vermis of the Cerebellum, which controls muscle development and balance, was one-third the size it should be. Rare doesn't even begin to cover the circumstance in which we found ourselves. I had never known anyone with either of these conditions, let alone both. I steadied myself in preparation for my next question: *Is my son going to die?*

That is the moment in which James Taylor aimed and fired. I had just asked the hardest question of my life, and his answer was NOT what I was looking for...

CHAPTER 1

THE BALLAD OF BLIND MELON CHITLIN'

I wasn't the most popular kid in the West Jones High Class of 1987. In fact, I was a bit of an outcast. Don't get me wrong. I wasn't getting shoved in lockers or anything like that. Our school, like all schools, was divided into tribes. They were, in order of social dominance, the In Crowd, the Out Crowd, and Our Crowd. We were the straggler calves of the herds who never quite fit into anybody's pasture. We were the social equivalent of Switzerland in WWII. We interacted with and had friends on all sides, but we hardly got invited to participate in their activities. We were neutral, and we were okay with that.

In the greatest of all decades, the eighties, when Bill Cosby was still America's Dad, and not America's creepy, inappropriate Uncle, you needed one or more of the following to be considered cool:

1. Money
2. Designer clothes
3. A badass ride

4. Athletic ability
5. A satellite dish in your yard big enough to double as a cereal bowl for God

Haircuts were another indicator of one's coolness. For young men, mohawks were big (thanks, Mr. T), as were high top fades, and rat tails. And for the young man who knew not only where the business took place, but also where the party was, there was the mullet. The ladies were all about the big hair. Some girls jacked their hair up so big and full that sometimes they would discover entire families of small animals residing within their freshly permed locks.

I was partial to the mullet. It seemed like a natural, low-maintenance way of making a statement. Sadly, my hair has always been both wavy and dry as a popcorn fart. So when I grew it out, it became quite frizzy. One might even go so far as to say fluffy. I had a fluffy mullet. My natural, low-maintenance statement was *I am a big, fat loser with the hair of a low-budget clown.*

To say I grew up in a poor family is the granddaddy of all understatements. My parents worked very hard but made precious little money. Thus, designer clothing was nowhere to be found in my closet. My classmates were wearing Members-Only jackets, acid-washed jeans, Vans, Calvin Klein, Polo, and whatever the overpriced trendy *brand du jour* was. I had boot-cut Levi jeans and whatever shirts happened to be on sale at Rose's or TG&Y, two department stores that kept those of us who couldn't afford to shop at the mall from going to school naked before Walmart came to town.

I also ran a deficit in the vehicle department. The cool kids were driving Mustangs, Trans Ams, and a beautiful assortment of pickups from Ford, Chevy, and Dodge. For most of my high school years, I drove a 1974 Chevrolet Caprice Classic. If you Google that particular make and model, you will see some beautiful photos. Know this: mine didn't look like that. My Caprice was green. It wasn't even a normal shade of green. It was a weird green that was a mixture of bird poop and the contents of a diaper worn by a baby who finished a massive meal of nothing but strained peas earlier in the afternoon. Well, most of it was green.

At some point in the life of this car, before my father handed it down to me, the passenger side door suffered some sort of tragedy that caused it to be removed and replaced by a door purchased by Dear Old Dad at a local junkyard. The door was a perfect match, except for one thing. It was sky blue. Sky. Damn. Blue. To make matters worse, my beloved father handed this chariot down to me in the prime of my teenage dating years. My friends and I called it *The Green Bomb* because *Ugly Ass Steaming Pile of Crap* took too long to say.

The Bomb had an added feature that no other vehicle I have ever seen had. There was a hole in the floor of the passenger side. I don't know why. It just did. Sometimes, if we were on a long roadtrip, the carpet would drop down the hole just enough to touch the tailpipe, and it would begin to smoke. So we poured whatever we had on it to keep it from bursting into flames. "Pour another coke on the fire," became a familiar rallying cry in the front seat.

I was never much of an athlete, either. As far as I know, I still hold the record for the most strikeouts in a single season for my county in Little League. After being turned down for the football team in elementary school due to lack of size, strength, speed, agility, and the ability to walk ten feet without tripping over something, my friend Greg suggested I join him in the high school band. Much to the chagrin of my parents, I declared myself a drummer and set about making sure the adults in my life required a daily dose of some sort of *nerve pill,* as my mom used to say.

It was in the drum corps that I found myself. It was there that I discovered a deep love for music. It could be because banging on that drum touched me on some primal level. Perhaps it was because, in my first year, we played an excellent marching version of Toto's *Africa.* Maybe it was because that band uniform was the nicest set of clothes I owned. Perhaps it was the people making music with me. The truth is, it was probably Jimmie.

Like my friend Greg, Jimmie Smith and his twin brother, Johnnie, had joined the band a year before me. When Greg suggested I join the band, part of his sales pitch was the other members of the corps. He assured me that a good time awaited with the wide assortment of misfits that made up the rhythm section. He also told me about a class called Percussion Ensemble, which was basically an hour-long practice session for drummers, in which next to no practicing ever took place. The class took place during the latter two-thirds of the ninety-minute lunch period, which meant we would have lunch, followed by an hour of first-class time-wasting every day. That's a sales pitch you don't walk away from.

It was during my first session of Percussion Ensemble Goof-Off class that Greg introduced me to Jimmie and Johnnie. I was drawn to them immediately.

They were exceptional drummers, and as it turned out, excellent musicians in general. They would go on to play piano, bass, lead guitar, rhythm guitar, harmonica, and more. Jimmie was also a singer. I found them both intriguing and amazing. Why? Because they were both blind. Don't worry about backing up to the beginning of the paragraph. You read it right. Jimmie and Johnnie Smith, the twin brothers who, at the time, were playing cymbals and bass drum, respectively, and marched during every halftime show, band clinic, and competition, had been blind since birth.

The Smith brothers were the first people I had ever known with special needs. Of course, we didn't call it *special needs* in the eighties. They were disabled. Only they weren't. They hated that word, and they taught me to hate it, as well. Nor were they *differently abled, handicapable*, or any other cutesy buzz phrase made up by people with no challenges to make themselves feel better for being normal—which, by the way, is another word I have grown to hate.

The Smith boys required no label. They were Jimmie and Johnnie, pure and simple. Sure, things were different for them. They lived in a world they had never seen, and that presented specific challenges, but they just rolled with it. Their blindness was a big deal to everyone except the two of them. They didn't want special treatment or consideration, and a sure-fire way to piss them off was to give them the impression that you felt sorry for them. They needed help, and they were not bashful about asking for it, but they wanted you to help because that's what friends do, not because you took pity on them. They wanted to be part of the gang, nothing more, and certainly nothing less.

Every person has specific points in their life where they can point to a day and say, "that's when everything changed." For me, one of those days was the first day of school, Tuesday, September 6, 1983. That's the day I walked into band class with my friend Greg, who promptly introduced me to other members of the drum corps.

There were Glen and Dave, two guys who had attended my elementary school but were two years ahead of me. Jason was the sole player of the triplet drums, due to his extreme talent, but also because he was the largest member of the drum corps and the only one who could handle the weight of that particular instrument while marching. Van, the prettiest guy in school, who was the spitting image of Peter Reckell—the actor who played Bo Brady on *Days of Our Lives*—was a bass drummer. Girls swarmed around Van like flies, and the rest of us tried to stand close to him in hopes of catching one he had rejected. Jamie played the cymbals, next to Johnnie. Greg played the bass drum along with Jimmie, Derek, and Mark.

As the rookie, I got assigned snare drum and miscellaneous percussion, which includes any percussion instrument without a drumhead. Triangles, woodblocks, claves, maracas, tambourines, and any number of noisemakers no self-respecting teenage boy trying to score points with chicks would be caught dead playing outside the band hall.

After pleasantries were exchanged, Mr. Meador, the band director, stepped up to his podium, and we got down to business. My first impression of Jimmie and Johnnie was something along the lines of *dang; these blind dudes are better at this than I will ever be.* I'm not going to lie. It was more than a little deflating watching two guys who couldn't even see the instruments they were playing keeping better time and getting more notes right than me, a guy who was looking at both the drum and the sheet music.

Once I got past thinking ridiulous stuff like *I wish I were blind so I could play like that*, I decided to spend a little time getting to know them. It turned out to be one of the best decisions I ever made. A friendship was born that day that is as alive and well as I write about it as it was during those crazy years in high school. I came to love Jimmie and Johnnie like brothers, and we were all the best of friends, but there was something special about my friendship with Jimmie.

Over the years, the two of us would become inseparable, growing a friendship that was different from the relationships I had with other friends. Most bonds are historically based on common interests, shared goals, or just plain old geography. With Jimmie, the foundation was different. Our foundation started and ended with trust.

There are different levels of trust. There is the kind where you trust I will be on time to pick you up for dinner. Another form is the trust in which you reveal some secret to someone and know it will go no further. A father trusts that the young man standing nervously at the door will treat his daughter with the kind of respect she deserves as they drive away for a date. A bride trusts that the man standing with her at the altar isn't just repeating back words to the preacher, but is legitimately making a vow before God that he will indeed love her until death do they part. Children trust their parents to provide and protect them. Parents entrust their children's safety to the teachers at their school.

Jimmie and Johnnie trusted me with their safety and well-being. For the first time in my life, I had became entrusted with responsibility for other human beings. They trusted me to get them safely across campus, or a street, or a golf course (yes, in fact, they DID play golf), or the lunchroom at school. They trusted me to help them organize their money into specific folds for different denominations so they could pay without allowing total strangers to have free reign in their wallets. They truly trusted me. I did not realize how deep their trust went until years down the road. I didn't think about it in those terms. I was just having a good time with my boys, but our good times involved a few unusual extracurricular activities.

To be a true friend, and a trusted member of the inner circle of Jimmie and Johnnie, was about more than just drinking beer, dipping snuff, and playing music. It was about looking out for them. It was about being a *Seeing-Eye Human*, as Jimmie dubbed me early on. Neither of them got a service dog until we were all in college, and they didn't need one. They had me and a couple of other friends who would take a bullet for them. When it was time to move, those of us who accepted the challenge would say, *grab some shoulder*, at which point they would place a hand on our shoulders, and we would navigate them through whatever terrain was before us.

It was through this process that Jimmie and I truly bonded. We talked about everything under the sun while we were walking hand on shoulder down the street, through the mall, or wherever we felt like wandering. Sometimes we would go to the park, or a crowded restaurant, or anywhere a large crowd might be so we could practice our technique. Sometimes we did it because it was the eighties, and the sight of two young men walking side-by-side, with the one on the right gently resting his hand on the shoulder of the guy on the left, made people uncomfortable—and we couldn't get enough of that.

You earn trust by showing trust. It wasn't fair for Jimmie to place his life in my hands if I couldn't return the favor. I struggled for a while to find a way to show my friend that his trust in me was reciprocal. Then one afternoon, as we were driving South on I-59, I had an epiphany.

Interstate 59 carried people blissfully past Laurel, MS, a city that at the time was famous for two things. There was the *hospital S curve*, a poorly designed curve in front of the hospital, which, due to a high embankment, was the source of approximately eighty-six traffic accidents daily, and the never-to-be-forgotten smell of the Masonite plant. Masonite, for the carpentry-impaired, is a type of wood manufactured by pressing together several different types of wood, using fresh pig manure as an adhesive. I am one hundred percent certain that this is not the actual recipe, but it sure smelled like it. Jimmie and I were cruising down this lovely highway listening to Randy Travis' *Storms of Life* cassette, when out of nowhere, Jimmie blurted out, *What's it like to drive?*

If you've never tried to explain the experience of driving to a blind man, you should give it a try sometime. After several attempts, all starting with *Well...* and ending with *Uhhh...*, I threw in the towel. *Screw it! I have no idea how to explain it. What if I just show you?*

After a second or two of silence, while my friend contemplated the utter ridiculousness of what I was suggesting, he gave a well-thought-out, carefully worded response to my question: *Hell yes!*

He shouted so loud that the sweet sound of Randy begging the operator to get him back to 1982 got lost entirely to our joint excitement. Things were about to get real!

The first session of Jerry's Driving School for the Blind took place in the parking lot of our high school on a sunny Thursday afternoon following band practice. I recruited Greg Holifield, the guy who made this madness possible in the first place with his invitation for me to join the band, and Mase Blackwell, the third member of Jimmie and Johnnie's inner circle and Seeing-Eye Human squad, to help set up the perimeter. We needed to clear any non-essential vehicles out of the driving course.

When word got out about what we were planning, it didn't take a lot of convincing to get our fellow bandmates on board with clearing a path. We patiently waited for Mr. Meador, and any other adults we feared might be small thinkers who would try and end this display of bravery and inclusion to go home, and then we got started.

This particular day, I wasn't driving the Green Bomb. I was in my uncle's truck. I was living with my uncle and aunt at the time (we'll get to that later), and he was kind enough to let his nephew borrow the truck because, you know, I was responsible and all. I put Jimmie under the wheel, and we spent some time going over the cockpit. Gas, brake, steering wheel, gear stick, turn signals, radio; we covered all the essential stuff. I decided to skip the lesson about the speedometer, due to the fact we were in a parking lot, and let's face it, what good is a speedometer to a blind guy?

Once Jimmie was comfortable with the functions of the various pedals and switches, I gave him the go-ahead to fire it up, and I assumed my position as First Officer/Navigator. I had thought about this quite a bit and had determined that the best place for me to be during this historic moment was on the running board on the driver's side. Hanging on to the outside of the truck while Jimmie lost his driving virginity gave me the advantage of being able to grab the wheel in the event a sudden shift in direction became an issue. From this vantage point, I could also get an unobstructed view of the parking lot and any potential victims who might wander into our path.

My job was simple: Jimmie would do the driving, and I would be the original GPS unit. I would instruct him to go, stop, and turn left or right. His job was to listen intently and follow all directions from the navigator hanging outside the window, while keeping his promise that no matter what happened, he would not—under *any* circumstances—floor it. The No-Floor-It clause was the only rule we discussed. It was the only rule that mattered. If he gave it too much gas, and I lost my grip, God only knows where the truck would end up, or how many vehicles, people, and chicken houses would be in the wake of the death and destruction he left behind. Worse yet, I and I alone would be held accountable for the explanation of what in the actual hell just happened.

When he put the truck in drive and released the brake, I saw someone become completely free. The kind of freedom a young man feels when he gets behind the wheel unsupervised for the first time. The freedom one can only experience while looking through a windshield. Jimmie later shared with me that he had dreamed of that moment for years, but never thought he would find someone *stupid enough to let him try it*. Little did he know, when he met me, a new level of stupid had entered his life.

As we worked our way around the parking lot that day, I was beaming like a proud father, joy streaming from every pore. My friend was driving. My blind friend. My disabled friend, who told his handicap to kiss his ass at every opportunity, was currently living the dream of every fifteen-year-old male in America. He was behind the wheel, and he was in control. He was alive! Our friends in the parking lot were amazed, and more than a little terrified. They would learn to ignore these little escapades over the years. Whatever Jimmie wanted to try, I did my best to make it happen. He wanted a normal life, and I was hell-bent on helping him have one.

My friendship with Jimmie was a non-stop series of adventures. We played in bands together. He manned the keys and took care of vocals. I handled the drums. Following in the footsteps of our heroes, we made up comedy skits that were absurdly funny, yet so incredibly inappropriate that the thought of those old cassettes finding their way into the wrong hands sometimes makes me wake up in a cold sweat.

We drove around listening to music, or the comedy tapes of Richard Pryor, George Carlin, Eddie Murphy, and Cheech & Chong. We could accurately recite nearly every joke or skit any of those comic geniuses ever recorded. One, in particular, had a significant impact on us. Cheech & Chong had a bit in which a fictitious blues singer named Blind Melon Chitlin was appearing in court. If you're unfamiliar with the work of Mr. Chitlin, here is a little piece of his work:

Goin' downtown, gonna see my gal/Yeah, I'm goin' downtown, gonna see my gal/gonna sing 'er a song/gonna show 'er my ding dong...

The bit in question entailed Blind Melon appearing in court on charges of sexual harassment. The judge asks, *Mr. Chitlin, how do you plead?* Chitlin replies, *I plead insanity.* The judge asks, *Insanity?* And in a punchline that would get Cheech & Chong canceled on social media and run out of the country on a rail today, Chitlin says, *That's right, insanity. I'm just crazy about that girl!*

I never said it was highbrow comedy. It was the low-hanging fruit comedians aim at fifteen-year-old boys, and we couldn't get enough.

Jimmie could do the best impersonation of that character. Somewhere along the way, I began to refer to him as *Blind Melon Chitlin*. To this very day, when he calls me, those words appear on my screen.

We were living our best life at the time, and the sight of me walking along with Jimmie, his hand on my shoulder, bobbing and weaving our way through the world became a perfectly normal sight around the campus of West Jones High. We could also be found at the bowling alley, or on a basketball court, and yes, driving around the school with me hanging on the outside of the truck like a misplaced hood ornament. Once we even gave archery a shot, but after losing half my arrows, and having a huge red spot on his wrist where the string kept popping him when he released it, Jimmie decided once was enough for the blind Robin Hood routine.

It wasn't all fun and games. As you might imagine, Jimmie had a lot on his mind, and he needed an outlet for his stress and frustration with life. We became each other's sounding board.

His parents were divorced when we met, and his Dad had remarried a woman Jimmie couldn't stand, who came with a son he could stand even less. To be fair, nobody could deal with the stepbrother. He was a spoiled, entitled, manipulative little turd. And those were his useful features. I'm sure he grew up to be a fine young man or, at the very least, a model prisoner somewhere.

My parents divorced two years after that first Percussion Ensemble class. It was loud, ugly, and much too public for my taste. The fact is that my mom was having an affair. That, in itself, would be bad enough, but the person she chose to have a relationship with was one of my high school teachers. That sort of thing doesn't stay off the radar in a tiny little town, especially when other teenagers, who live to be in and around drama, catch wind of it.

Dad found out about the affair from, of all places, the trash. We had a fifty-five-gallon drum in our backyard, like all families in our area. It was there for the sole purpose of burning garbage. The environment was on its own in the eighties. Dad was an over-the-road truck driver and was gone for long stretches at a time back then. On one of the rare weeks when he got to spend more than a few days at home, he was taking some trash out to the burn can. When he dumped it into the can, a letter fell out of the bag and onto the ground. It was clearly in Mom's handwriting, written to her lover.

The details it provided about the relationship left no doubt about what was happening, why it was happening, and with whom it was happening. She was pleading with the man to leave his wife so she could leave Dad, freeing them up to be together. I know all this because Dad shared the information with me later that night. I guess he just needed to tell somebody. From that day to this one, I wish he had called a friend. There are some things a fifteen-year-old kid doesn't need to know.

Allow me to hit the pause button for a minute and explain that I love my parents dearly. They were good, decent people who made a few awful decisions in their lives. I have often said they were much better parents *after* the divorce than before. I long ago forgave my mom (and my teacher) for the pain I dealt with due to her infidelity and told her so directly. As I've grown older, and I hope wiser, I've also come to understand her situation at the time. I have been married to Daphne for twenty-seven years at the time of this writing, and I've made some monumentally stupid mistakes myself.

I can see, looking back, that Mom was lonely. Dad traveled for weeks at a time, and when he returned home, he was too tired to do much other than sleep. He would hang around a few days and then be off on another run. That life must be hard on a woman. Add that to the fact that their favorite little *uh-oh*, me, caused her to have to get married at 16, and immediately become a wife and mother. And then, of course, there was the fact that we were so damned poor. Add all that together, and it's a recipe for disaster in a marriage.

When the divorce started getting ugly, which didn't take long at all, the games began. Both parents wanted to make sure my sisters and I were on their side. I have never talked to my sisters about it, so I don't know how much they knew at the time, but I knew everything that was happening. When I was with Dad, he would unload on me about all the horrible things Mom had done, and when Dad wasn't around, I got the dirt on him from Mom. Neither of them seemed to care at the time, but I believe it is closer to the truth to say they just didn't understand what they were doing to me emotionally. Much like the incident that set the wheels of divorce in motion in the first place, I was a dumpster fire.

As I said, I made my peace with Mom and Dad a few years later, and we all went on to have a wonderful relationship. Before I lost them, Mom and Dad became friends, maybe for the first time in their lives. Our family got blown to hell for a while, but in the end, we were all good. I will never say what they did during those years was right, but I *will* say I understand.

Along with the usual problems of teenage boys, I would bend Jimmie's ear about these things. God bless him, he must have been sick to death of hearing my tale of woe, but he never acted like it. He was there, listening. Jimmie did not give commentary unless I asked him for advice. He didn't try to solve my problems; he just let me purge myself whenever I wanted, and let me tell you, I had to purge myself *a lot.*

Kids are kids, and teenagers are teenagers. Our younger selves had the potential of being heartless little bastards on occasion. When word of my mom's affair got out, it was big talk around the school. Knowing that one of our teachers was involved made it a much bigger gossip topic. Sometimes they talked about me when I wasn't around. Sometimes they whispered as I walked by. Sometimes they just said it to my face. There were fights at first, but I eventually learned to ignore it. I kept my head down for a couple of years until some other scandal came along, and my family drama fell off the top of the charts.

Jimmie defended my honor on more than one occasion. If he heard somebody say something about my situation, he would unleash his red-hot temper on them. The great thing about watching Blind Melon Chitlin rip somebody a new one was they just stood there until he finished telling them what he thought.

Nobody wanted to be the person who punched the blind man.

To keep me sane during those crazy years, I developed a bit of a devilish streak. I've always loved a good joke, and Jimmie was such an easy target! There were times when we were walking I would lead him straight into a pole, door, bench, or a car, just to remind him who was in the Captain's chair. Then there was the time I convinced him to throw a penny at the metal window blinds in our classroom while our Senior English teacher, Mrs. Arrington, was speaking to the class about some classic piece of literature we were studying.

I told him I would let him know when she wasn't looking, so he could chuck the coin across the room to the blinds, with the intent of disrupting everything with the loud faux cymbal crash that was sure to follow. Of course, I waited until she was looking directly at him before I gave him the sign. She was not amused. Then there was the day we were walking down the crowded hallway to class when I dared him to pinch the butt of the hot cheerleader walking in front of us. Jimmie would do just about anything on a dare, so he dutifully reached his hand out and grabbed a handful of the left cheek of our school's quarterback—who was also not amused!

I admired Jimmie and Johnnie as much as I loved them. They had every right to be angry at the world for their situation, but they were not. They had every right to expect special consideration from those of us who called ourselves their friends, but they didn't. There was no reason whatsoever for them to expect to be treated like the rest of us, but they did. They knew the areas where they required assistance, and they were okay with asking for help and taking advantage of it.

But beyond that, they expected us to treat them like everyone else. I admired them for that because it allowed us to be *regular* teenage idiots. Their love for getting out in the world and having fun pushed me to do the same at a time when I would have preferred to go home and curl up in a fetal position. I'm grateful to them for that. And in my grown-up role as Grayson's dad, even more so.

As I look back on those early years with Jimmie and Johnnie, it is clear to me that even back then, God was working in my life in a sneaky, yet effective way. I was laughing my way through the teenage years with them, but I was also learning some profound, meaningful lessons.

Habits were formed. Belief systems developed. I was learning patience and perseverance. I was learning how to stand up for those who are different; to see the world as the beautiful work of art God intended it to be, even if it sometimes feels blackout dark. I was being groomed for an even greater adventure. One that would not fully reveal itself until two years after the Y2K scare caused half of the world's population to soil their pants simultaneously.

CHAPTER 2

THE STUPID LEADING THE BLIND

My adventures with Jimmie carried over from high school into college. There we continued our Batman and Robin routine until I made my first big adult mistake and took that semester off that so many have taken. You know the one. The semester where you declare a moment of respite from higher education, only to look up twenty years later and realize you forgot to go back. Before my lifelong break started, our streak of getting away with everything but murder came to a screeching halt one day in the name of love. Before it was over, both of us came very close to being kicked out of school altogether. All because Jimmie got himself a girlfriend.

Jimmie was smart as a whip, but all through high school and into college, he struggled with history. He struggled with it because he hated it. I appointed myself his tutor in high school. We would spend hours leading up to exams with me pacing around the room notebook in hand, repeating facts *ad nauseam* until he could regurgitate it back note-for-note. Then we would take the test, usually passing with flying colors. Two minutes after leaving the class, Jimmie would pull an invisible handle in his brain, and flush every ounce of his newfound historical knowledge down the drain. Memorization may be the lowest form of learning, but it has saved the educational life of many a struggling student throughout the years.

And so, it came as no surprise when we launched the higher portion of our education, that Chitlin was no fan of a course required of all freshmen called Western Civilization. He hated it with every fiber of his being. Two weeks into our first semester, he announced he was going to drop the class to save his GPA. I wasn't having it. I told him to grow a pair and let Batman handle it. I devised a plan. It wasn't a good plan by any stretch, but there are times in life where a man will convince himself that a bad plan is better than no plan at all. Men are stupid like that.

Step one of the plan required us to sweet-talk our way into the professor's office. There we convinced her the best course of action to keep Jimmie from showing up in her class every semester for years to come. She should allow me to give Jimmie his exams. Through crocodile tears that filled puppy dog eyes, we explained the plight of this poor, wretched handicapped student. He wanted nothing more than to receive a high-quality education, but would surely be hindered in his efforts without the assistance of his trusted Seeing-Eye Human. To my amazement, she bought the BS we were selling as though it were the purest of gold. And so I added *test-*

giver to my ever-growing list of duties as Jimmie's main dude.

The plan was quite simple. Jimmie would feign interest and type feverishly on his braille typewriter during class. It didn't matter what he was typing. He was the only person on campus who could read it anyway. He could be writing a dissertation on U.S. Grant's leadership techniques during the significant battles of the Civil War or jotting down a recipe for three-alarm chili. It just didn't matter. I would actually *be* interested and take voluminous notes during her lectures, which were as interesting to me as they were boring for the blind man.

On test days, I would take the exam and ace it like a boss. I had my shortcomings in my youth, but when it came to being a student, I was a total badass. Nothing brought me more pleasure than seeing an A or a one hundred percent mark on a big test. It gave me the same satisfaction I get now when I mow my lawn. I appreciate any activity that allows me to do something, then turn around and immediately see the fruits of my labor. That feeling served me well in school, in bands I would later be a part of, in my career in radio, and in my stand-up comedy.

Before we get to stage two of the plan, I want to point out—in Jimmie's defense—that he did his part in all this. He studied with me the same way he did in high school. I paced and lectured, he listened and regurgitated, but that's where the similarities ended. In high school, the teachers read the questions to Jimmie and wrote down his answers. Our college Western Civ plan found the two of us in the professor's office, me doing the asking, and then writing down the correct answers, whether he got it right or not. True or false and multiple-choice questions involved a complex series of toe and finger taps. There was also a complicated series of fake coughs and sneezes to direct him to the correct response, just in case someone walked in while we were cheating his way through freshman year.

Flawless is not the word I would use to describe what was happening, but it *was* working. That is until Blind Melon Chitlin met a girl and fell into a severe case of puppy love. She was fun to hang with, she made him happy, and I was thrilled for them both.

A code is an integral part of a friendship. Bros before Ho's, Fries before Guys, Captain Jack Sparrow's pirate code, whatever. It's a line in the sand that is never, EVER crossed by anyone who vows to abide by it. In this particular case, the code was simple. I help you cheat your way through a class you hate, and we both take that secret to our graves. At the very least, we make it to the day after graduation. It was simple and easy to remember. At least I thought it was.

Then Jimmie Smith, my best friend and confidant, my super cool blind friend, my inspiration, my good and faithful keeper of secrets, decided the best way to get past second base with his newfound love was to share a secret with her. He would show her how much he trusted her, thereby melting her heart and removing all resistance to his romantic advances. And that's how he came to let her in on *The Great History Caper*. He told her EVERYTHING, right down to the signals.

When he told me of this egregious infraction, I forgave him immediately. I wanted to strangle him with my belt, but I forgave him. If he trusted her that much, I figured I should give her the same consideration. One month later, that whole *strangle him with my belt* thing became a much more viable option. It would be easy. He would never see it coming. Literally. These were the thoughts in my head as he explained how he had royally angered the girl of his dreams. To this day, I don't know what he did. I'm sure he told me, but the next words out of his mouth made my brain vapor lock, and I have blocked that part of the death of his great romance out of my memories.

She ratted us out, he said, lowering his head into such a position that the belt would slide right over. *They want to see us in the Dean's office*, I heard him say as the leather cleared the first two loops and I began to plan my future on death row. *What're you in for?*, the leader of the Aryan Nation would ask through his gold-plated grill. *I killed an old blues singer for a violation of the Bro Code*, I would reply, as I counted the cigarettes I would be using to hire bodyguards to stand outside the shower for the next fifty years.

Returning to the scene at hand, I looked at Jimmie like a puppy looks at television, eyes wide and head slightly tilted to the right. He couldn't see the face of the man who was currently contemplating his violent, gruesome demise, but he knew what I was thinking.

I don't know how he did it, but Jimmie went into the inquisition first, and when he came out, we were in the clear. We were on probation, but we were in the clear. I never asked him what he said. I didn't care. I had not been that scared since the night my friend Ralph and I were picked up by the police for violating curfew, because our ride was late picking us up after we went to a Civil Air Patrol meeting in junior high. That is the only time I have ever been in the back seat of a cop car, and I hope at the end of my days, I will still be able to say that.

Somehow, Jimmie had convinced them that the plan was his, and I was just being a good friend by tagging along. He had to go back and take all the exams again. In the most exceptional example of poetic justice I have ever seen, they chose the person who would be the reader of questions. That person was the young woman who rolled over on us. The ex-girlfriend. The traitor. The daughter of a motherless goat. Jezebel herself. When Jimmie dropped that nugget on me, I could not help but smile as I put my belt back on, and silently bid farewell to Dewayne and his fellow Nazis on Cell Block D.

CHAPTER 3

WHEN JERRY MET DAPHNE

In the early days of my college career, I stumbled upon a part-time gig at a local radio station. They hired me to work the six to midnight shift every Tuesday and Thursday night on WBSJ. This small-town Country station sat High atop Buffalo Hill, in the bustling metropolis of Ellisville, Mississippi. They hired me because I had experience.

My experience consisted of a whopping six weeks working for WLAU-AM. That station sat in the front bedroom of a house that was one strong gust of wind away from being a pile of scrap lumber, in Laurel, Mississippi. I eft that station after the third consecutive week of trying to cash my paycheck, only to watch the tellers call a huddle before giving me my meager wages.

The drunk guy who owned the station wasn't much of a money manager. The trick was to be the first employee to reach the bank on payday. After that, getting your money was a crapshoot at best.

During my truly embarrassing first days as a DJ, I found myself in a new band. My friend Glen Musgrove, whom—you may remember—was part of the drum corps when I first joined the marching band in high school, assembled the group to play at a festival. It went well, so we decided to keep going. I was in hog heaven. My life was full of music, and as far as I was concerned, music was life. Shortly after putting our group together, I decided to take that semester off. A word of advice to the high school or college student who may be reading this: *do not take a semester off!*

Odds are you will never go back. When you step off that college campus and into the real world to take that well-deserved break from education, the real world has a gravitational pull that is nearly impossible to escape. Things happen. Some are bad, some are good, and others are phenomenal. However, they all work toward the single goal of stretching that semester into a year, a decade, a lifetime. I'm not complaining by any stretch of the imagination, but that's what happened to me.

I met her at a band rehearsal. Glen and I had rounded up a great group of musicians to form the band. We called ourselves *Sonja Street and Backstreet.* Sonja was our lead singer. Her voice could melt butter. We made her our lead singer after one performance. She was and still is a fantastic singer. She was on her way to Nashville, and we were ready to tag along for the ride. We rehearsed as though we were playing Madison

Square Garden every time we got together, and if I may be so bold, we were better than good. We were damned good.

We had everything you could ask for in a band. A beautiful lead singer with an even more beautiful voice, killer musicians, great harmonies, and a smartass who loved nothing more than being in front of a crowd to fill gaps on the mic between songs. As the least talented musician in the group, I volunteered as tribute when we realized we needed that smartass. I could carry a tune okay, and I got good at singing harmony through the years, but my true love was that microphone.

Making an audience laugh, cheer, and get ready for whatever was next; that was my thing. That band became everything to me. It didn't matter whether we were on stage or rehearsing. When we were playing, I had everything I ever wanted. Then she came to rehearsal, and all that went right out the window.

Her name was Daphne. She was Sonja's first cousin. She was also a fan of my radio show. I had been promoted from nights to afternoons several months before. I was partnered with the funniest human I've ever known. His name is Ken Stokes, but his fans know him as *Cousin Ken*. How funny is he? At his mother's funeral, we were standing in the cemetery saying our goodbyes when Ken's sister walked up and asked him if he had paid the preacher. Ken never missed a beat. He looked at her and said, *Pay him? Hell, I thought he liked Mama!* That's a level of funny that can't be taught.

Together, we were *The Cousin Ken and Jerry Show*. We had no clue what we were doing. The people we worked for at WBSJ had no clue what we were doing, either.

What we DID know was that we were funny on the air together, so we just went with that. Daphne had been listening to the show for a while. When Sonya told her I was in her band, she wanted to come to rehearsal to hear the group and to meet one of her favorite DJs.

The first thing I noticed was her height. For reasons even I don't understand, I've always had a thing for short girls. Short equals cute in my book. Daphne was four feet, eleven inches of solid gold cute. The second thing that got my undivided attention was her lips. She had those sexy, pouty, Hollywood starlet lips. The kind of lips you want to kiss the second you see them. She was dressed in a pair of faded shorts and an oversized t-shirt. It was the early nineties, and she looked the part. Her hair was long and curly, pulled up and to the side. Her eyes were a strange shade of grayish-green. I don't remember the brand of the shoes she was wearing, but they were the same shade of bright white as Luke Bryan's teeth.

She was an absolute goddess, and she scared the hell out of me. Not because she was the most beautiful thing I had ever laid eyes on, but because she was only four-eleven, weighed about ninety pounds, and was wearing braces. I thought she was no more than fifteen or sixteen years old, and I knew the last thing I needed was to get caught giving googly eyes to a fifteen-year-old. I was twenty-one, and even in Mississippi, that's frowned upon.

During rehearsal that night, her age came up in conversation. I seized the opportunity to find out if I was breaking state law in my mind just by looking at her and told her my guess at her age. To my delight (and my total doubt), she told me she was nineteen. That's when I accused her of being a liar, less than two hours after meeting her. She bounced over to her purse, almost as if she were skipping. Or floating. I was pretty much done at this point. I knew she was going for her license. The fact that she was moving in that direction told me she was telling the truth, but my heart was trying to kick a door open, and before I let it happen, I had to know. She was telling the truth. She *was* nineteen. The girl of my dreams was old enough to be in my thoughts without me needing to go to confession, which would be weird anyway because I'm a Baptist.

I had known Daphne for approximately two hours at this point, which, coincidentally, was the same amount of time I had been completely in love with her. When I saw her date of birth on her license, I stepped away from that door I was holding closed, and it flew off the hinges. It was over for me. I had experienced a couple of nasty breakups in the preceding few years, and vowed it would take a woman an eternity to get her claws into my heart again. Daphne took it entirely out of my chest in what is undoubtedly the shortest eternity on record. I was hers twenty seconds after she walked into rehearsal, and she didn't even know it.

When the rehearsal ended, I was falling all over myself trying to impress her. I prayed it was working, but I had no idea how to read her. It felt like she was flirting with me, but her personality was so big and bubbly, it almost seemed like she was flirting with the world and everyone in it. With my previous train wrecks, I was trying to be as cautious as a man can be when he runs headfirst into his destiny.

We were playing our first real gig the next day, and I invited her to come watch the show. I mean, she should be there to support her cousin, right? She said she would try. I heard *no* in sixteen different languages and all caps, but I was strangely okay with that. I knew we were meant to be together, and if I had to do some extra work to make that happen, then so be it.

She put her perfectly tanned legs inside Sonja's car and closed the door when it was time to go. I waited for them to get out of the parking lot before turning to Dave, our drummer, and saying, *I'm gonna marry that girl.* He laughed. I laughed. He went back inside. I stared at the road and planned my future.

CHAPTER 4

CALLING DR. LOVE

Well, of course, there was a boyfriend. How could there not be? I didn't even bother to ask, I just knew. I could not fathom a world in which a woman that beautiful, with that personality, didn't have a guy following her around like a lost dog. When Sonja informed me there was another rooster in the hen house, I took it in stride. I didn't even consider it a setback. After a little detective work, I found out everything I needed to know about my soon-to-be romantic rival. A good soldier doesn't go to war without a battle plan, and you can't plot out your campaign without vital information. What did he have that I didn't? What were his strengths? What, if any, were his weaknesses? Where was he vulnerable?

He looked like Tom Cruise had a baby with Justin Timberlake. I was not going to beat him on looks. He had been in the army, but so had I, so in the category of who loved America more, we were at a draw. He was quite stylish. If you go back to the list of things that were required to be cool, he checked off every single one, damn him! He gave the impression that he had money, but I wasn't sure. Her family loved him. Like L-O-V-E-D him. Daphne lived with her grandparents, and from what I had learned, good ol' Memaw was already picking out china for them.

The battle was shaping up. It was not going to be easy. He was holding all the cards, but I didn't care. I was in love. I was determined to do whatever it took, short of becoming a story for the future Mr. and Mrs. Pretty Man (remember that creeper with the mullet who used to stand by your car with a guitar and some flowers?). I would leave the battlefield with my pride intact. Everything else would be left on the field. I saw very clearly what I was up against and was surprisingly unfazed.

She was out of my league, and I knew it, but I continued to move forward. The battle between the Abercrombie & Fitch model and the broke-ass redneck with his best pair of white leather high-top Converse shoes for the heart of the fair maiden would be one for the record. I vowed it would end with the peaceful transfer of affection from The Pretty One to yours truly.

What I lacked in fashion, money, and looks, I attempted to make up with charm. It was my secret weapon. It had served me well through the years, but now I would need to reach deeper into my well of charm than ever before. Daphne was not a prize to be won. To earn a place by her side, I was going to have to resort to some proper old-fashioned wooing. And if wooing was what it took, I resolved to be the wooingest wooer in the history of woodom. Provided, of course, that she showed up for that performance.

We were halfway through our soundcheck when I saw her. She was floating again. She drifted effortlessly across the grass of the park, where we prepared the launch of our music career on the back of a flatbed. It was the annual Day in the Park, or the Possum Festival, or whatever it was. She was in white shorts and a tee, hair in a glorious ponytail, carrying a Styrofoam cup full of ice from Sonic. In the years since that day, I have purchased enough of that ice to sink a battleship. That girl loves to eat ice from Sonic. When she got close enough to the stage, I said something brilliant like *look who decided to join us*. I don't recall my exact words. I may have said *if you can't get here on time just get here when you can*, or some other classic statement from the annals of true romance.

Then the most amazing thing happened. She looked at me and smiled, took a piece of ice out of her cup, and threw it at me. My heart ricocheted off the top of my skull when it leaped at this juvenile act of young love. My future Queen was flirting with me! I played my guitar and sang that day as if I were giving the last performance of a fifty-city tour. I'm pretty sure my feet never once touched the two-by-six boards that made up the floor of the flatbed. And through it all, only one thought was on my mind: Let the world championship of wooing begin. Somebody tell the Fat Lady she's on in five! The Pretty One was about to lose his girl.

Stage one of Dr. Love's battle plan was friendship. I needed to cool my jets and become a friend. That way, I wouldn't scare her off by saying something stupid like, *do you believe in love at first sight?* I threw water on the fire in my heart and settled into my role as crazy old Jerry, the DJ.

She spent time with the band for Sonja (or because she was defenseless against the power of my mullet), and during breaks or between sets, we would all sit around and talk. More precisely, she would speak, and I would listen. Remember, I was a badass when it came to learning, and at this point in my life, I was majoring in Daphne, with a minor in espionage. I soaked up everything she had to say. Her favorite music, food, movies, all of it. I was stockpiling ammunition.

I made my first move about a month after we met. Daphne was going to a concert with the Pretty One on a Saturday night and would be off the grid until Monday. She had mentioned in one of our conversations that she was a big fan of Jimmy Buffett. Sadly, her knowledge of his music was limited to his more mainstream songs. By that, I mean she only knew the music featured on his Greatest Hits package, *Songs You Know by Heart*. She struck a nerve with that morsel. I was the self-proclaimed King of all Parrot Heads, the name given by JB to his most dedicated fans. I lived and breathed the music of Buffett and had for years.

I stopped at Walmart on my way home from work on Friday and picked up the biggest pack of cassettes I could find. When I got home, I made her a bootleg copy of every Buffett album in my collection. Yes, I was stealing the man's music for my gain, but in my heart, I felt Jimmy wouldn't mind at all. Any man who could write *A Pirate Looks At Forty, Come Monday,* and *Why Don't We Get Drunk (And Screw)?* was obviously a romantic of the highest order. Buffett would jump at the chance to assist his biggest fan in the game of love, right?

Inside the jacket of the first cassette, I wrote a note. There was nothing overtly romantic about it. I simply told her I was providing this music as a remedy for a bad day. When things weren't going her way, she could pop one of these into the cassette deck. Then she could roll down the windows, and let Jimmy and the Coral Reefer Band take her to the islands for a while. *Charm, Baby. Charm.*

Phase two was a little more devious. I invited Daphne to come by some time for a tour of the radio station. She was fascinated by radio. I have learned through the years that many people share that feeling. When you live on the other side of the curtain as I do, you don't understand why the general populace oohs and ahhs when you tell them what you do, or when they recognize your voice and start asking questions. Those of us blessed to sit behind the microphone take it for granted most days. To us, it's just a room with a bunch of equipment. To the listener headed down life's highway listening, it is so much more than that.

We are your constant, albeit invisible, shotgun rider; your friend with no baggage—that dude that says the things you are thinking. I have been told many times that a show I was part of was a ray of sunshine during a dark period of someone's life. Listeners tell stories of how our music and jokes lifted them out of sadness or helped deal with a bout of depression. In a conversation I will never forget, a young man shared with me that some situation I was bloviating about convinced him not to take his life, and to seek the professional help he needed.

The effect those of us in this wonderful business have on those who are kind enough to give us their attention is often lost on us. We're just having fun and chasing a dream. Occasionally, someone reminds us that what we do can be, and often is, important. Daphne was one of those people. She loved the music, the stories, and the overall mystique of radio. She was a fan, not just of the *Cousin Ken and Jerry Show*, but of the industry in general. Did I take advantage of that to try to get her a little deeper into my world? Damn right, I did! #notsorry #noregrets

To my pleasant surprise, she accepted the invitation and showed up early for her tour. I showed her around our meager building and tried to sound like I knew what I was talking about when she asked questions about the equipment. I introduced her to my co-workers, and like everyone else she ever met, they fell in love with her. She has that effect on people. God knows she had it on me. When the tour ended, we sat down in my office and talked for the rest of her lunch hour. She was a dental hygienist at the time, and the war on tooth decay waits for no man. Sadly, when the hour was up, she had to get back to work.

The rest of my day was shrouded in a cloud. If you haven't picked up on it yet, let me break it down for you. I had it BAD for this girl. Don't let my bravado fool you. While my plan seemed to be working, I was terrified that any time I was with her would be the last. She had the Pretty One, after all, and even though it was plain to see she wasn't exactly all in on that relationship, she *was* still in it. I had her attention. The bigger question was, could I keep it?

I got my answer the next day when I was in the production room, recording a commercial. The receptionist called to tell me I had a visitor at the front desk. I walked to the lobby, and my heart smacked the top of my head again when I saw Daphne. It was time for another lunchbreak, and she wanted to talk. I invited her into my office again, and we had the first of what would turn out to be tens of thousands of long talks about life, the universe, and everything. She was very open about the fact that she was picking up vibes from me, and I was very open about the fact that she was right. Although I decided to hold back on telling her I pretty much had our entire lives planned out already...

That approach seemed a little intense at the time. I did, however, let her know in no uncertain terms that I was doing everything I could think of to make sure I was at the front of the line when she decided to change partners. I also made sure she was aware that I was perfectly content in the meantime to be her friend if that was the only way to have her in my world.

Over the next few weeks, we shared many lunches in that office. Daphne opened up to me about her relationship with the Pretty One, and how she wasn't exactly happy with their situation. It seemed to me that she felt trapped. Everybody loved the guy. Her family and friends thought they were perfect together. On paper, it looked great. In reality, things were quite different. He was incredibly jealous, overbearing, demanding, and disrespectful. To be fair to the Pretty

One, we were all young and stupid. None of us knew what we were doing. As crazy as it sounds, I tried to counsel her on ways to make their situation better. I loved her, and I wanted nothing more than for her to be happy. If fixing her relationship with him was what she needed, I was willing to grin and bear it and try to help. That's what I kept telling myself, anyway.

She was quite candid with me through it all. She thought she was in love with him, but clearly, something was going on between us, and she was torn. She was trying to figure out what she wanted. For a while, she was getting the best of both worlds. The Pretty One provided entertainment and stability, and all the things that make up the *surface* of a relationship. I was the heart and soul she desperately wanted in her life. Someone who cared about Daphne the person, not Daphne, the arm candy. I wanted to know about her hopes and dreams.

She shared with me years later that I was the first guy who actually cared about her feelings. She had dated several guys and had discovered that age-old pattern of men who have but one thing on their minds. When she ran into me, she did not know what to make of it. She told me I scared her because no guy had ever placed her on a pedestal before. She didn't know how to handle it. Looking back on it now, it's funny to me that she read that deep into what was happening. This was NOT part of Dr. Love's battle plan. It was just happening. As *Air Supply* so eloquently put it, I was *lost in love*, and for the first time in my life, I was putting someone else's happiness in front of my own. Stealing her from The

Pretty One was no longer a priority. SHE was the priority.

Having said all that, every man has his limits, and I reached mine two months down the road. Our conversations in my office at lunch every day were the highlight of my life, but I wanted more. I wanted dinner conversation. I wanted to take her out into the world and experience it together. By now, Dr. Love's Battle Plan was pretty much forgotten. She was all I thought about, and it was becoming more and more painful to bare my soul to her for an hour, only to send her back to him. I rode that wave for as long as I could, but the day came when I could no longer handle the status quo. It was the day of the *Great Cake Speech*.

She went by the station for her lunch visit, but she didn't find the happy-go-lucky DJ she had come to know. She found a sad, forlorn guy with a heavy heart who had reached an impasse in life. I sat her down and threw every card I had on the table. *You can't have your cake and eat it too*, I said, sounding very much like my Mamaw Clark. *I can't do this anymore. You HAVE to know how I feel about you by now, and this thing, that isn't a thing, we're doing isn't fair to me or the Pretty One.*"

I didn't call him that to her face. I used his name. Since all this happened another lifetime ago, his name is irrelevant to our tale. I could tell by the look on her face that she was not expecting this. The light in her eyes faded. Her body language shifted. She was stunned. To be honest, so was I. I had just told the girl of my dreams she had to choose between a guy she had been dating for several years and me. He was light years ahead of me in the game. There was a genuine possibility this would be the last conversation I would ever have with her. Was I really that strong? Hell no, I wasn't!

When she drove away that day, I felt like I had just cut out my own heart with a rusty blade. I was sure I would never see her again. I told myself it was better for both of us. I said to myself that if she chose him, we were not meant to be, and I would be fine. Then I looked in the mirror in the men's restroom just before going on air for my show, took a deep breath, and said *You, my friend, are full of crap!*

Several days went by before I saw her again. Once again, I was in the production studio recording a commercial for some car dealer who was having a *Push It In, Pull It In, or Pray It In Sale.* Car dealers are always right on point with a snappy name for a sale. It's a *Jesus Saves And So Can You Weekend!* I was toiling away recording some such nonsense when the receptionist called and said I had a visitor in the lobby. I put my shoes back on and started down the hall. I don't know why, maybe it's the backwoods country boy DNA in my system, but I don't like to wear shoes when I'm working. I want to get comfortable. It helps me be creative. If you ever catch me in the middle of some big project with our show, a client, or our station, you will most likely see me in socks, my shirt untucked, hat on backwards, looking like I just woke up from a two-hour nap. That's me, in all my redneck glory.

At that moment, I had no clue I was not just taking a short walk to the end of that hallway. I was taking the first steps of a journey that thus far has carried me through four states, seven radio markets, nine stations, ten morning show partners, one bout with cancer, the loss of my parents, an almost-divorce, three kids, and an adventure with kid number three that none of us saw coming.

Standing in the lobby of that little station *High atop Buffalo Hill* in Ellisville, Mississippi, was Daphne. I don't remember what she was wearing that day, but she was holding a bag containing two foot-long chili cheese conies, and two medium drinks from Sonic. I didn't say a word, and neither did she. There was no need for words. Those beautiful eyes told me everything. She had made a choice, and she had come to seal the deal with a chilidog.

CHAPTER 5

ONE ROLL OVER THE LINE

Relationships are hard. You don't just get involved with the girl of your dreams. You get the whole enchilada, which comes with the girl and everyone in her circle of influence. Friends are easy unless you're an asshat. As long as you are treating their girl right, they tend to give their blessings early in the game. Family, however, is another story. With Daphne's family, Stephen King could very well have written the first few chapters of that story. Or Rob Zombie. They hated me from day one. I don't mean the kind of hate where they just look down on you because they do not think you are good enough for her.

They hated me with the sort of hate Bruce Willis' character, Jimmy "The Tulip" Tudeski, from the movie *The Whole Nine Yards*, hated mayonnaise. *I'm gonna keep the Coke and the fries, but I'm gonna send this burger back. If you put any mayonnaise on it, I'll come over to your house, chop your legs off, set your house on fire, and watch you drag your bloody stumps out of the house. Okay, Pierre?*

That kind of hate.

I mentioned before that Daphne lived with her grandparents, M.L., and Voncile Davis. The elder Davises had five children, Nonnie (Daphne's mom), Charlotte, Rud, Frankie, and Phil.

Each of the adult Davis children were married or divorced, with children of their own, most of whom were within a year of Daphne's age. Every one of them, with the exception of Daphne's older sister, Stephanie, and her Aunt Charlotte, appeared to wish fiery death upon me and all that I stood for the first time we met.

The Davises were a proud Southern family who had once owned a thriving family business in the oil industry. That business had experienced a horrific downturn in the two years before my first appearance at their door. The details of the crash are lengthy and complicated, and I would be happy to bore you with the ins and outs, but frankly, I never truly understood what went wrong. You see, I was an outsider. As such, I never got invited to the group therapy sessions the men of the family would hold every Sunday afternoon after their family lunch, which followed the family trip to church. Those meetings were filled with talk of who screwed up what, how they could have done things differently, and plans for financial recovery.

Even though I felt as welcome as a festering cold sore the first year or so, I was enthralled by these meals. Mrs. Davis, like all proud Southern matriarchs, would lay out a spread fit for a king every week, and every member of the family was expected to be present. She demanded nothing less. As a broke, single guy who was practically starving on the sad salary of a small-market DJ, and whatever funds our band made on weekends, I began to look forward to Sundays at Memaw's. I would start thinking about Sunday lunch around Thursday each week.

Memaw was the name of honor the family used for Mrs. Davis. All of them, even her own children, called her Memaw. Neighbors called her Memaw. The preacher called her Memaw. The man who owned the store down the street called her Memaw. I called her Mrs. Davis, partly out of respect for my elders, but mainly because she scared the hell out of me. I was never quite sure if I had the right to use the family terms of endearment.

She hated me above all the others because she was the President of the Pretty One's fan club. She loved that boy, and had gotten quite comfortable with the thought of him being her grandson-in-law. She was quite surprised when Daphne announced he would not be coming to Sunday lunch anymore. She was even more amazed when she found out who would be taking his seat at the table.

I often wondered why the Davis family had decided to go into the oilfield business, because—whether they knew it or not—their real talent lay in cooking. This family could prepare food fit for the finest of restaurants. Every week I would be amazed at the feast before us. Pot roast that required no chewing was a staple. Mashed potatoes and all manner of vegetables (homegrown, of course) adorned the counters in the kitchen.

The men of the family had constructed a smoker in the backyard that was practically a walk-in. Every time I pulled into the driveway, the sweet smell of smoking meat would wrap around me like a warm hug. Ham, turkey, chicken, and sausage (both pork and deer) were always hanging in the *Mother of All Smokers*. They were champions of the grill, as well. Rud, especially, could make a meal Gordon Ramsey would be proud of on a charcoal grill. I always admired the way he refused to use a gas grill. I hated gas grills. My dad was a charcoal man, and he passed that love down to me.

I'm older and lazier now, so my deck is adorned with a very nice gas grill. Still, there's something about building your own fire, and making food art with it, that appeals to me on a cellular level. I spent a considerable amount of time hanging around the grill with Rud. I figured out early on that he didn't hate me; he just didn't want the rest of the family to know he didn't hate me. I didn't blame him. He had no idea how long I was going to last, so why bother with defending his position on whether I belonged at the table?

One of my first memories of the Davis family still comes up at least once a year, when we get together for holidays, weddings, or funerals. I call it *The Brown 'N Serve Incident,* and it left its mark on us all. It was Sunday lunch number three. I had grown somewhat comfortable breaking bread with a group of people that did not want to break bread with me. I had also gotten a little bolder about going back for seconds. And thirds. The food was some of the best I had ever eaten, and I only had one shot a week to stock up until next time.

No matter what was on the menu, Mrs. Davis always had a piping hot basket of Brown 'N Serve dinner rolls. These were served in a wicker basket with a lovely white towel across the top (who *were* these people?). I have had a lifelong love affair with carbs, and those rolls were my favorite source. On the day of the incident, I arrived hungry and decided to carb up. To be honest, I don't know how many rolls I ate that day, but it was more than I should have. Then I committed a sin so unforgivable it is spoken of in hushed tones to this day. The fact that it was thirty years ago doesn't cushion the deep feelings it conjures. The family still speaks of it reverently, even though one of the participants in the incident has since passed away.

I don't know what I was thinking. My parents made their mistakes in my childhood. Still, they certainly raised me with better manners than I exhibited when I reached under that towel and ate *the last roll*. In Southern culture, you do not eat the last anything unless the head of the household offers it to you. At the very least, you have to say *Hey, y'all, there's only one roll left. Does anybody want it?* Neither of those options applied here. I took it. I knew better, but I could not stop myself. I quietly returned to my seat and finished my meal. Then I took my plate to the kitchen, feeling great about being full and getting away with first-degree culinary murder. That's when I heard the deep, gruff voice of Mr. M.L. Davis—who, in the three weeks I had known him, had said a total of six words to me—ask the entire household, *Who ate the last roll?* My heart sank.

In my mind, I could see myself in a small, dark room, a single, seventy-five-watt bulb hanging from a long cord over the table. Mr. M.L. was leaning over the table, giving me the full good-cop/bad-cop routine, minus the good cop. *Was it you?* he asked, knowing damn well it was. *I want a lawyer*, said the soon-to-be convicted roll thief.

As I left the interrogation room in my head and returned to the kitchen, I was standing over the sink, water running, frozen in place. I was just about to rinse my plate and put it in the dishwasher when he asked the question. My first thought was to keep my head down, ride out the silence, and pray he would realize it was just a roll, and therefore was no big deal. However, it was not just a roll. It was HIS roll, and he wanted it. Apparently, he was one Brown 'N Serve dinner roll shy of being satisfied with his Sunday lunch. No one said a word.

I could hear crickets chirping. The clock on the wall next to the stove stopped ticking. I had never been around someone with the power to freeze time. It felt like an hour passed. The silence began to drive me mad. I suddenly felt compassion for the subject of *The Tell-Tale Heart*. When I could no longer take it, I spoke up. My voice sounded like the cracked, sheepish uttering of a 4-year-old with a face covered in chocolate as his father inquires who ate the Snickers bar he left on the counter.

I wanted to say, *It's a freaking roll, old man! Relax*, but I knew better. He could make my life a living hell, and I desperately wanted him to like me. He did not. Much to my chagrin, my brutal honesty did not change things between us. The man was livid. Sunday lunch was going down in flames, and the new kid with the bad shoes and mullet was to blame. The outsider. The interloper. The Mayor of Trash Town. The roll-stealing, boyfriend-replacing little sumbitch who showed up for lunch with his precious granddaughter in a green car with a sky-blue door.

It was not the last time I would be thrown out of the Davis' beautiful home on a sunny Sunday afternoon, but it was the first, and it was a bit of a moment. I'd never been asked to leave anywhere before, but here we were. Mr. M.L., standing by the empty roll basket staring a hole deep into my soul, and me, plate in hand, water running, shame emitting from every pore. I contemplated a lengthy, contrite apology. Nothing came out. Words don't have a habit of escaping me. I generally keep a good supply corralled up like lambs headed to slaughter. But there was something about the gaze in that roll-deprived old man's face that said it would be in my best interest to tap out, thereby living to fight another day.

The next time Mr. M.L. invited me to get the hell out of his house came about a month later. A friend had given me a dog he was unable to care for, and since it was a teacup chihuahua, and Daphne was a huge fan of little dogs, I gave it to her as a gift. She fell in love with Sassy the moment their eyes met. *Charm, baby. Charm.*

What neither of us bothered to consider was the immediate future. Mr. and Mrs. Davis were more than happy to provide room and board for their granddaughter, but they were not running a damned kennel. I know that, because when Daphne and I took Sassy to meet her new landlords, Mr. M.L. looked at the dog, gave me an all-too-familiar look of disappointment mixed with frustration, and said, *I'm not running a damned kennel!*

This meeting happened on Thursday afternoon. My ejection from his property came the following Sunday. Rest assured, I kept a distance of at least three feet from the roll basket, so that was not the issue. To this day, I don't know what set him off. He directed his rage at Sassy, who was hanging out under the sizeable farm-style table waiting for someone to drop anything that might be edible. He looked down at this goofy-looking dog, hit me with the eyes of death, and announced to all within earshot that it was time for me to take my little dog and get the hell out of his house.

This time, I felt my father's temper welling up inside. I knew beyond a doubt I was about to say something so disrespectful to this old geezer while sitting at his table that I would never be allowed to come back. I would probably have to change churches before everything was said and done. My filter had a massive crack in it in those days, but Daphne's cooler head prevailed when she touched my hand and said through her embarrassment, *Come on, let's go.* I complied.

I sat down under the wheel of my Chevy and slammed the door so hard the carpet dropped into the hole in the floor, setting me up for another floorboard fire on the way home. Daphne must have apologized thirty times between the living room and the driveway, but I was not having any. I told her I would never darken their door again, knowing that was a lie. My pride was severely bruised, and I needed to pout for a minute. Then I had to figure out what to do with the Taco Bell mascot in the passenger seat.

The Davis family. We got off to a rough star, but we grew to love and respect each other.

CHAPTER 6

THE ALMOST NOT-SO-HAPPY ENDING

So went my life for the next 18 months. I would show up for lunch, they would allow me to sit at their table, but they would pass their disdain around like mashed potatoes. The women in the family created an excellent game they liked to play, in which they would regale me with tales of The Pretty One. Pretty One this, Pretty One that. It drove me insane, but I never let it show.

One Sunday, to let me know exactly where I stood, Mrs. Davis invited him to church. She insisted he sit next to her on the pew that was known to all who entered Evergreen Baptist Church as *Memaw's Pew*. The Davis family were all members of the quaint, little church and had been for years. When business was good, I imagine they were in the top one percent of donors to the plate.

When you have that kind of history in a tiny church in Shubuta, Mississippi, you get to claim a pew. And woe be unto the stranger who wandered in for a visit and plopped down on someone's designated pew. I am convinced there are people in hell right now who made an honest attempt at meeting God, but were so turned off by the *Who is this heathen sitting in Old Man Jenkins' seat?* looks they received, they never set foot in a church again.

I cannot honestly say his presence didn't bother me. The fact is it pissed me right off, which put a significant damper on my worship experience that morning. I sat there through the service, staring at my Bible, seeing the preacher's lips moving but not hearing a word. I was too busy wondering what I would do if he showed up at Davis Manor for lunch. I decided I would shove Brown 'N Serve rolls down his throat until he choked, then make a loud noise that would scare Sassy so bad she would *drop the chalupa* inside one of Mr. M.L.'s slippers. The thought of him sliding that big, calloused heel into a fresh chihuahua turd made me smile. You shouldn't hate somebody that much, especially when you are sitting behind Old Man Jenkins at church.

In September of the following year, Daphne went to Virginia to spend a few weeks with her mom. That's my version of the story. Daphne will tell you we had a big fight while her mom was in town, and I sent her away.

She had moved into my apartment a few months earlier because her relationship with her grandparents had hit the skids over me. I hated it for her, because she loved them dearly, especially Mrs. Davis.

I wanted to fix things between them, but only one side of that battle gave a hoot in hell about what I thought. Besides, since the night they had fought their final round about my worthiness to be in her life, the woman of my dreams was going to sleep with her beautiful head on my chest every night. While I knew what we were doing was not socially or spiritually acceptable, I very much enjoyed having her there. Frankly, I was in heaven.

As it turned out, it was more like *Heaven Lite*, where happiness tastes great but is less filling. I had never cohabitated with (or *shacked up* with, as Mamaw Clark put it while telling me how awful my situation was between bouts of praying for my certainly damned soul) a woman before. I found it strange. She wanted stuff organized. A place for everything and everything in its place. She didn't like my Clint Eastwood photo from the set of *The Outlaw Josey Wales* that hung in a place of honor in my living room. She was OCD. How had I never noticed THAT little detail?

I was, and still am, a walking tornado, leaving a wake of half-filled glasses, empty plates, and shoes in my wake. She was spoiled rotten, courtesy of Mrs. Davis and her free-flowing checkbook. I was all about compromise. Daphne was all about getting what she wanted when she wanted it, how she wanted it. We were oil and water. We fought like cats and dogs. So yes, I will admit now in front of God and everybody that in fact I did send her away with her mom. I thought the break would do us good. I knew it would be great for me. I needed a break from what seemed like one long argument broken into smaller pieces that had been rocking on for weeks. She was not happy about it, but she agreed to go.

It took about five minutes after I knew she had crossed the county line for me to realize I was an idiot. I had heard the saying *do not cut off your nose to spite your face* my entire life. I had no clue what it meant until that first night alone in my apartment after she left.

In the early nineties, long distance was still a thing. Today if you send your girl to Virginia with her mom so you can have some peace and quiet, only to realize that peace and quiet was not really your thing, you just pick up your cell and call. Back then, you had to pay extra for the privilege of talking long distance. For the record, the distance between my hometown of Soso, Mississippi, and wherever the hell they were in the hills of Virginia, is vast. I called her every day. We talked for hours. I became concerned I was going to bankrupt the company I worked for because I always called from work. After a few weeks, I began to think I needed a new plan.

I needed someone to help me clear the cobwebs in my brain. I needed someone I could trust without question to give brutally honest answers to brutally honest questions. It was time to call in the big guns. It was time to talk to Uncle Ronnie.

CHAPTER 7

TIME TO PUT A RING ON IT

Vernon Ronnie Clark is my mother's baby brother. He is the youngest of my grandparents' three children. Because Mom had me when she was so young, there is only a twelve-year difference in our ages. I don't know why, but he always treated me more like a little brother than a nephew growing up. We were very close when I was younger. When he met and fell in love with his future wife, Darla, they would occasionally take me on dates with them, when they were going to a movie. I have fond memories of a movie called *The Legend of Boggy Creek* because it launched a lifelong fascination with Bigfoot for me. To this day, I still research the 'Squatch every chance I get, and I love to see stories of sightings. This piece of cinematic artistry was the first movie I took in with the future Mr. and Mrs. Clark.

When my mother took a swan dive off the deep end for a few years, I eventually reached a point of feeling as though I had no choice but to leave home. The horror of dealing with her escapades had reached the apex of its trajectory, and I could not deal with it anymore. I had bounced around for a while, spending time in the homes of various cousins. My favorite cousin, Brenda, gave me a place to crash for a while, as did her sister, Wanda. They were awesome, but they had families of their own by then, and while they would never have said it, I knew I was a third wheel they did not need. So I kept moving. I even convinced the parents of the girl I was dating at the time to let me stay in their home for a time. I was essentially homeless.

Then I had an idea. It was a horrible idea, but it sounded good at the time, and boy, did it look good on paper! My girlfriend's parents had recently moved into a new home, leaving their old one unoccupied. I rounded up a couple of friends, both dropouts—one from high school, one from college—and convinced them to rent this house with me. We would be the three amigos, living large in a home you had to leave the paved road to find. I'm not sure how I thought we were going to survive. I was a Domino's Pizza delivery driver at the time, and my bi-weekly checks barely covered the gas I was using to sling pizzas all over town, much less cover one-third of rent and utilities. None of that mattered. I just wanted a home to call my own.

Into this looming catastrophe came Mamaw Clark, who had realized something wasn't quite right with my mom. She found out things that were going on in our home that mortified her, and she did not know what to do with the information. Mamaw knew what I was planning to do, and she knew it was going to end badly for me. She also knew at that point in my life, she wasn't exactly my favorite person. I had tried to explain some of the things I was dealing with. She wrote me off as an angry teenager looking to get out of the house and not have to take orders from anyone. When she realized I was telling the truth, she did the only thing she could think to do. She called Uncle Ronnie. She knew how close we were, and that I would listen to whatever he had to say.

They met up, and she filled him in on the things she had discovered. My mother had written checks on my account. Checks she stole from me. Checks that bounced as though they were made of rubber. She had taken my grandfather's shotgun, which he gave to me before he died. He had five grandsons, and for some reason, he wanted ME to have his single-shot twenty-gauge shotgun. It was my prized possession, right up until the day she took it to a local pawn shop, hocking something I would not have sold for a million dollars for a lousy 30 bucks. When I walked in and saw it gone from my gun rack, I asked Mom whether she had seen it, and she said no. That was just one of many, many lies she told me during those crazy years. She also hocked some jewelry Dad gave her as a gift.

To make matters worse, she tried to make it look like someone had broken into our home to steal that jewelry. She even called the police to come out. They didn't believe her. They couldn't prove she was filing a false report, so there was not much they could do, other than telling my grandfather what they thought was happening. Many more incidents were to come. Incidents that dazed and confused us all, and drove me further away from her.

My mother was not evil. She was sick. The person she was before would not recognize who she became during my high school years. It was clear something was wrong, and while I wanted it to be something simple like *she's just a crazy bitch, and I never noticed it,* even my under-developed, hormone-addled teenage brain could see the problem ran much deeper than a personality issue.

My Aunt Elsie made it all make sense one day. Elsie was my dad's older sister and possessed no filter of any kind. Her thoughts became her words so fast, I'm not sure even SHE could stop them. Aunt Elsie was a drama queen long before that term became a thing and a busybody of the highest order. She was also one of the kindest, most caring people I ever had the pleasure to know. She and my mom had been great friends before Mom's wires got crossed, and she missed their time together. Aunt Elsie spent a great deal of time trying to figure out what was happening to her sister-in-law. One day, we were having one of our prolonged discussions in the local donut shop she managed. During that talk, she gave me the details of the only theory that ever made sense to me. Aunt Elsie blamed it on the accident.

When I was twelve, I was in the car with my mom; both my sisters; Mom's best friend, Aileen; and her four children. We were on our way to our house after the moms had done some shopping. The weather was terrible that day, and during our drive, a torrential downpour hit with the fury of a category five hurricane. I had never seen it rain that hard. The road disappeared in the deluge of water just as we entered a curve, and I learned what it feels like to hydroplane at sixty miles an hour. The car went entirely around at least three times and only stopped because we slammed broadside into a tree on the side of Highway 28.

Before the accident, I had been sitting in the front seat between Mom and Aileen, holding Aileen's youngest daughter, Jessica, who was no more than a few months old. It was the early eighties. No seat belts, no baby seats, no safety features whatsoever.

When she realized the situation was about to go from bad to worse, Aileen pushed me into the floor to protect her child and me. When I sat up moments later, I checked the baby in my arms. She was fine. Aileen was in the passenger seat, shaken but seemingly uninjured. Mom, however, was no longer under the wheel. I looked out the front windshield to see if maybe she had gotten out of the vehicle. She had not. Then I heard a moan. It was the kind of cry you hear from someone who is in unfathomable pain, but also somewhat unconscious.

I looked behind, and to my horror, I saw her. The impact had thrown her from under the steering wheel and over both the front and back seats. Her body became a missile that struck the rear windshield, spreading a million shards of shattered glass over the trunk lid. She was sprawled across the trunk. Her legs were about a fourth of the way inside the car, dangling over the back seat. There was so much blood, I remember being confused about whether I was looking at the front or back of her head when she raised up.

The gash in her scalp took nearly a hundred stitches to close. The rest of the passengers suffered injuries ranging from scratches and bruises to my little sister Sandy's shattered femur. The front seat had collapsed on her legs when the tree stopped our spinning, and she spent the next six months in a body cast. Mom carried a great deal of guilt about what had happened, but the fact is we had blown a tire at the exact moment we went into that curve when the rain was at its hardest. The result would have been the same, no matter who was driving.

I believe she suffered some sort of traumatic brain injury in that accident, the kind that changes your personality. I am no doctor, so my belief on the matter holds no value whatsoever. I just know she went run-over dog crazy for the better part of a decade and then reverted to her old self. It took several years for me to be able to forgive her for the wildfire she started in my life, but forgive her I did, and I told her so. For the rest of her life, our relationship was as good as any mother and son in history.

I was standing in the kitchen at my girlfriend's house when I got the call. I was being summoned to Uncle Ronnie's house the following afternoon. There was no option to not be there. His tone was strangely serious, and I knew something big was about to go down.

The next afternoon, after school, I went straight to his house on the outskirts of Soso. As was, and still is, his fashion, he spoke plainly. There would be no beating around the bush this day. He told me everything he had learned from Mamaw. My heart sank. Why is it that children feel shame and guilt over the actions of their parents? I was embarrassed, angry, heartbroken, and thankful, all at once. Even though we were discussing topics I did not want to confront, it was a massive relief that I was discussing them with someone who had my best interests at heart. Uncle Ronnie wasn't just telling me what he thought I wanted to hear, and I was happy he had gotten involved. This man loved me. I could see it in the pained expression on his face. He was hurting *for* me and *with* me. After all, the person who was the nucleus of my pain was not only my mother, she was his sister.

He told me he knew about my plans to move into the house with my friends. Then he spent a few minutes telling me that while he understood what I was trying to do, I wasn't ready for it. It was going to end with me in debt, or worse, dropping out of school to work more to make rent money. He had discussed my situation with Aunt Darla, and they had reached a conclusion I will never understand or be able to repay.

They wanted me to move in with their family. Their young daughters, Kristi and Heather, would move into a bedroom together. I would take up residence in the middle bedroom, where I sleep even now when I'm home for a visit. They wanted me to be a part of a grounded family. They wanted me to be a part of *their* family. I accepted the offer immediately. I didn't know what life in the Clark household was like, but it had to be better than anything I had going at the time.

I spent a couple of years living with the Clarks, and they were the happiest years of my life up to that point. Kristi and Heather became much more than my first cousins. They became my sisters. My relationship with Ronnie and Darla is hard to pin down. They are my uncle and aunt, but also my older brother and sister, surrogate parents, and dear friends. I would fall on a grenade for any member of that household.

We are as close now as we were then. My children look at Ronnie and Darla as a third set of grandparents. We vacation together. We spend holidays together. My birth parents will always be Mom and Dad, and my love for them knows no bounds, even though they are no longer with us. Still, when I think about my *family*, my thoughts immediately go to a couple who didn't have to do a damn thing for me but chose to do everything.

And so, I found myself once again at their front door on a cool September evening. I had come for life advice, and they were happy to hear me out. I knew I would get straight talk, with no fluff, and that is what I needed. I was contemplating a move that would be a game-changer, and I needed someone to tell me whether I was on the right track, or had lost my mind because I missed my girlfriend.

I showed them the ring I purchased earlier in the day. It wasn't much, to say the least. I had gone to Kay Jewelers with every penny I was able to scrounge. I purchased a set of wedding bands AND an engagement ring for a hundred and seventy-five dollars. It was the best I could do.

I told them about my situation with Daphne. They met and fell in love with her the previous year, so it wasn't as if I was proposing to some stranger. I told them how much I missed her and how I was on the verge of putting a company out of business with my daily long-distance calls. I mentioned I had decided living without her was not an option. Then, the question. Was I doing the right thing? Uncle Ronnie looked at me for a brief moment, answering my question with a question of his own. *Do you love her?*

He asked the question feeling confident he knew what I was going to say. *More than anything* was my reply, and I meant it. Then he gave me the kick in the pants I needed to get off my ass and make something happen. *Well, you're not getting any younger!*

And that is how I wound up standing in the baggage claim area at the Jackson-Medgar Wiley Evers International Airport in Jackson, Mississippi, waiting for my future Queen to step off the plane. I had saved more money for a few weeks after my meeting with the Clarks, and I bought her a one-way ticket home. When she rounded the corner and caught my eye, I proved to her without a doubt that my cheesiness knows no bounds. In my hand was a cardboard sign that said *Welcome Home, Daphne!*

She smiled when she saw my second grade-level handwriting and began walking faster in my direction. I motioned for her to stop, and when she was standing about ten feet away, I flipped the sign to reveal even more simple chicken scratch. In giant, bold letters, it read *Will You Marry Me?* She burst into tears as I dropped to one knee and held out that pathetic excuse for a ring. My tears held off until she said yes, reached for my hand to pull me up, and threw her arms around me.

The baggage claim area erupted in applause. The Queen had returned to her kingdom, and I had never felt so whole.

The best First Mate a Captain ever had!

CHAPTER 8

NOT EXACTLY CHARLES AND DI

By the end of the ninety-minute ride from the airport to our apartment, the wedding was all but planned. Notifications to the proper friends and family members had been made, and we passed giddy before we hit the halfway mark of the trip. It didn't matter that we had no money. It didn't matter who was happy and who was ordering a voodoo doll in my image. We had each other, and we had all the love in the world. What else could we possibly need?

Money. You need money to get married, although weddings were not the lavish, Royal Family-style events they are now back in 1992. Earlier this year, our daughter, Hayley, married her Prince Charming. Conservative estimates put the cost of their grand oceanside ceremony somewhere in the vicinity of thirty-five thousand dollars. The budget for Daphne and Jerry was three grand, which may as well have been three hundred thousand.

Tradition says that the family of the bride covers the cost of the wedding. That custom didn't take into consideration that the family of the bride wanted to see me drawn and quartered in the town square. We were on our own, and I was—in the immortal words of my Granny Broadway—*broke as a haint*. (*Haint* is Southern slang for a ghost, which has no visible means of support.)

Uncle Ronnie showed me how much he believed in our decision by co-signing a loan for me, using Daphne's Chevrolet Beretta as collateral. We had our money, and we were off to the marital races. Daphne, her sisters, and friends handled a great deal of the planning, with more than a little help from my cousins Wanda, Brenda,Glenda, and Tammy as well as Aunt Darla.

Being on a tight budget means you cut corners when you can. Daphne borrowed a wedding dress from our friend Joy, and it was pretty much the only decision we made that didn't end in some level of disaster. One corner we cut that probably should have been left intact, was the bridesmaid's dresses. Daphne knew someone who knew someone who had a cousin that was a seamstress. She made the dresses for the bridesmaids at a substantial savings, which is why we can't show our wedding video in polite company. She finally got the dresses finished a few days ahead of the ceremony, and there was no time for alterations.

Our wedding looked like Happy Hour at Hooters. Every single bridesmaid had a dress that looked like it was custom made for Dolly Parton. I'm pretty sure the inside of the First Baptist Church of Soso never had, and probably hasn't since, seen so much cleavage gathered together at once. It was an absolute boob fest. At one point in the video mentioned above, my friend Gerry Wyatt can be seen talking to another member of the wedding party. One of the ladies walked by with everything she had to offer on display. Gerry looked straight into the camera and said, *Did you see THAT?*

Another cost-cutting measure was the photographer. Daphne's family had a photographer that they had worked with for years. He cut us a great deal on the photos. Since we got four inches of rain on the day of our wedding, he waited until after the ceremony to shoot anything. He held us in the sanctuary of the church so long that Daphne and I completely missed our reception. If that makes you sad, don't let it. These days a wedding reception is a grand affair featuring great food, emotional first dances, a band or a DJ, and silly traditions like the groom firing his new bride's garter over his shoulder to designate the next brave soldier to fall.

In 1992, you got married in the church, then proceeded straight to the Fellowship Hall to have dinner. Catering was for the rich and famous. Our reception was catered the Deep South Baptist way, a covered dish potluck provided by family members. None of that mattered to the newly christened Mr. and Mrs. Broadway. By the time the marathon discount photography session was over, we had to settle for a plate Mamaw Clark had saved for us. We also got to watch the ladies of the family clean up the Fellowship Hall. Everyone was gone. No receiving line. No dollar dance. No first dance as husband and wife. Just an unceremonious bite of wedding cake and the sound of several brooms sweeping across the tile floor.

I should also mention that on the morning of our wedding, something went wrong with the *engine* in the Beretta that paid for this grand event. It was so bad, we had to borrow a car from Uncle Ronnie and Aunt Darla to go on our honeymoon. After we left the most anti-climatic reception in history, we got in our borrowed car, went to their house to change clothes, then stopped back by the church on our way out of town. Someone had to help finish cleaning up.

Little did we know that the comedy of errors that was our wedding day was but a glimpse of what God had in store for our future together.

Our honeymoon—and I use the term loosely—was a whole two hours away from home in Biloxi, Mississippi. We spent the weekend at the Royal D'Iberville Hotel on the beach. Okay, it was across four lanes of Hwy 90 from the beach. Okay, you couldn't see the beach because we were on the backside of the hotel. As a former boss at a radio station would say to me years later, *it's damned inconvenient being poor.* We didn't care about the hotel; we were too excited about getting to gamble at one of the recently built casinos. If you go to the Mississippi Gulf Coast now, you will swear someone picked up Vegas and moved it East. Casinos and massive hotels line both sides of the main highway.

When we arrived that rainy Friday night, there were four, all located on the beachside. The law said casinos had to be on the water, so they were built on massive pontoons at the edge of the shore. When Hurricane Katrina struck, she did a great deal of damage to New

Orleans (which got nearly one hundred percent of the press). You may not know, but that storm decimated the Mississippi coast and hundreds of miles inland. In doing so, she deposited a couple of casino barges in the middle, or on the other side, of the highway. To get the casinos back up and running as fast as possible, those laws were finally changed. Now you can't throw a rock without hitting a gambling establishment, hotel, or pawn shop.

Our first stop was Treasure Bay Casino, where I planned to complete our fairytale love story by winning enough money to set us up for a life of luxury. I had a crisp, new twenty-dollar bill set aside, and I was ready to do battle with the slot machines. Unfortunately, my blushing bride had forgotten her ID. Since she still looked like a fourteen-year-old, we were promptly asked to vacate the premises. We went back to our room to do what newlyweds do, but first, we made a decision that I believe to this day is the glue that holds us together. We sat on the bed, held hands, and prayed.

We were very open with God that we knew we had sinned, and probably would again. We asked not just for His blessings on our marriage, but also for His guidance. We prayed He would show us the path He wanted us on. We thanked Him for allowing us to overcome every hurdle that had been put in our way so far, and asked Him to never leave our side. It was an awkward, clumsy prayer. It was the first time I had ever said a prayer out loud that didn't rhyme. Looking back, it occurs to me that He was listening, and I think maybe those are the prayers He likes the best because awkward, clumsy prayers come from a place of pure honesty.

November 20, 1992

CHAPTER 9

THAT ESCALATED QUICKLY!

As foolish young couples often do, when Daphne and I returned in October from the airport the night of our engagement, we celebrated. *Perhaps,* I thought, as Daphne left the ER examination room to take a pregnancy test on New Year's Eve, *we may have celebrated a little too much.*

We had been married precisely thirty-nine days on New Year's Eve, 1992. We were living in the worst house that any newlywed couple had ever had the sorry pleasure of calling home. It was right in the middle of town in Soso, behind the chicken feed mill, which mercifully was shut down. I say mercifully because I grew up smelling the freshly brewed chicken feed that was made there, and it wasn't exactly pleasant. It was heinous. We moved into the place for one simple reason; *it's damned inconvenient being poor.* The lady who owned the property was so shocked to find someone willing (stupid enough) to rent the place, she only charged us a hundred and twenty-five dollars a month.

Next door to our little shack was the Soso water tank, the only water tank in Mississippi upon which no one had ever painted their name. On top of that tower was the town emergency siren, which sounded like every emergency horn you've ever heard in a movie, only louder. It had a soul-piercing scream that was a cross between the mating call of the Blue Whale and the guttural scream from that lady who became famous on the Internet when she fell to her knees in utter despair the night Donald Trump became president.

We called her Big Bertha. My entire life Bertha had stood watch over the three hundred and one citizens of my town. She diligently warned of impending disaster. She was also a key element in the education of those of us who attended Soso Elementary on the dangers of the Soviet Union. Once a month, like clockwork, someone in a position of great importance would, at his or her discretion, give Bertha a test scream. It was the loudest, most ear-splitting sound I had ever heard.

When Big Bertha roared to life, we had to stop and listen for about 15 seconds to determine our level of peril. A quick doppler effect, like the sound of a French police siren, meant that someone was in imminent danger of losing a chicken house, or maybe the family single-wide as a swirling vortex of death and destruction dropped from a nearby wall cloud to wreak havoc on all in its path. A long, solid blast meant that someone was in danger of losing a chicken house or the family single-wide to a fire, and all volunteer members of the volunteer fire department were to report for duty.

A series of short blasts, followed by the continuous banshee-like shriek of the Horn From Hell, meant the commie bastards in the USSR had finally launched the first strike, thereby assuring the mutual destruction of all mankind. Well, most of mankind.

Those of us who were lucky enough to be tucked safely under our little wooden desks, heads between our knees, would be fine. It was common knowledge back then that the most destructive and horrifying weapon ever devised was no match for a good piece of oak and a hard-plastic seat mounted on four aluminum legs. In the unlikely event the desk did not hold up under the stress of a nuclear blast, we were conveniently hunkered down in such a position that we could quickly kiss our asses goodbye just before our face melted.

About a week after moving into our little love nest death trap, with its leaking ceiling, and mold-covered back-bedroom walls, Daphne and I joined the Soso Volunteer Fire Department. Why wouldn't we? When Big Bertha went off at two in the morning, we were going to be up anyway. The damned thing was literally in our yard. When activated, it rattled the entire house. The first time it happened, we thought the house was going to collapse around us. Had that occurred, I have no doubt it would have done several thousand dollars in improvements to the property.

The scene repeated itself many times during those thirty-nine days. Big Bertha would break the silence of the peaceful Soso night with her wail of woe, and Daphne and I would each suffer a minor coronary event. Then I would crawl across the bed to the floor on her side, because our master bedroom was the size of a pizza box, and my side of the bed was touching the wall. Then we would throw on our clothes, jump in the car, and make the forty-two-second drive down the gravel road to the fire station, only to find the pumper truck had already rolled out.

How in the hell did the entire department—none of whom lived within two miles of Big Bertha—get dressed, get to the station, throw on their turnout gear, and leave before we could make it to the front door? Dedication, I suppose. Or excitement. There wasn't a lot to do in Soso, and getting to go fight a fire not only gave you a sense of pride but something to talk about the next day.

My last day with the VFD came in February when we were summoned to a brush fire in a local farmer's field. When we arrived at the scene, the pumper truck decided to take a well-earned break and refused to give us even a single drop of water. So we cut down some small pine trees, broke off some limbs, and beat the fire out. I quickly decided I could find some other way to serve my community than burning alive in a hayfield standing next to a truck filled with several thousand gallons of fire-killing water.

On day thirty-eight of our marriage, Daphne mentioned that she wasn't feeling well. She spent that night in the bathroom, throwing up everything she had eaten since birth. It was my first time seeing my bride in such bad shape, and I was seriously starting to worry. She was finally able to get some sleep around four in the morning. I thought maybe she had a touch of food poisoning.

When she woke up on New Year's Day, I asked her whether she was feeling better. She answered me by running back to the bathroom to resume the previous night's activities. She was weak and pale when she finally came out. She could barely stand. For the second time in my life, I was responsible for the safety and well-being of another person. The difference was that Blind Melon Chitlin never asked me to hold his hair while he up-chucked his spleen. I decided our best course of action was to get her to the hospital. By noon, I had convinced myself she was dying. I had never seen another person so sick.

When we arrived at the ER, the woman I loved had taken on the look of someone with a Fast Pass to a meeting with St. Peter. She was scared. I was trying my best to be the strong, supportive husband, but inside a four-alarm fire was raging, and my pumper truck was out of water. When the nurse asked her if she might be pregnant, I got a little angry.

I thought, *Can't you see this woman has Ebola? At the very minimum, it's Rocky Mountain Spotted Fever. Or maybe the flu.* This, of course, was before the time of Web MD, or any of the Iamgonnadie.com sites so many people use to misdiagnose their illnesses in present times. The only three diseases I was even remotely familiar with were the three in my thoughts now.

Well, there WAS that extracurricular activity when we got home from the airport, said a voice in my head that turned out to be my conscience. I was just panicking, I convinced myself. There was no way that I, the guy who finally broke the family tradition of the shotgun wedding, had carried it on to another generation without even knowing it. Was there?

When the reality of what might be about to transpire hit me, I began to experience what could be described as a nervous breakdown. I didn't want kids. I didn't want anything to do with kids. After the hell I had endured with my parents, which was still very fresh in my mind at this point in my life, the thought of being a dad filled me with a level of dread that is beyond description. I was finally free of all that. I had the perfect girl. For the first time in many years, I was truly happy. Our house was a steaming pile, and we were suffering from chronic poverty, but we felt like we were living the dream. It was her and me against the world, and I loved it. Putting a baby into that mix so early into our new life was going to be a disaster. The mere thought of it made me more than a little depressed. That is until the nurse came into the room with the results of the test.

Much to my surprise, when she informed us we were going to need a bigger house—preferably one with less mold and quieter neighbors—my heart exploded, but not the way I thought it would. Before the words had even cleared her lips, I was vowing internally to be the best damn Dad that ever changed a diaper. I was so happy I couldn't speak, and we've already discussed how rare those times are. I wanted to run out into the waiting room of the hospital and tell everyone there I was going to be a Daddy, but I couldn't seem to move. I just sat there staring into space, desperately trying to process my elation. I never wanted to be a Dad, until I found out I was going to be one.

We spent the next six months looking for a new house, buying baby clothes, bottles, a crib, and other accessories. We also embarked on a PR campaign to convince everyone we knew that our little one was a honeymoon baby. I don't think a single person bought it, but everyone was kind enough to play along.

Grayson loves his Hayley!

CHAPTER 10

THE QUEEN AND THE PRINCESS

Hayley Morgan Broadway arrived on Saturday, June 12, 1993. To my eternal sadness, Daphne went into labor while we were visiting my cousin, Kristi, in the hospital. Kristi was working her way through a bout of Bell's palsy, and since I considered her my baby sister, we dropped in on her early Friday evening. While we were there visiting, the contractions started.

Daphne had been experiencing Brooks and Dunn contractions for a few weeks, so at first I thought nothing of it. I know they are called Braxton-Hicks contractions, but Brooks and Dunn is so much more fun to say. I had been gearing up for my Dukes of

Hazzard-inspired drive to the hospital for a while, so I initially tried to convince her it was nothing, and we should just go home.

I had no intention of losing the opportunity to drive like a bat out of hell to get her to the hospital. I planned to take the last turn in a perfect drift that Vin Diesel would be proud of. I would hood-slide to the passenger side, fling the door open and carry her into the delivery room. There, Daphne would push three or four times, breathe as they taught us in Lamaze class, and *whammo*, the kid would be there. I estimated the entire process would take 40 minutes. Half of that time would be spent breaking the sound barrier in the Green Bomb, offering words of comfort to the patient while pouring Similac on the fire in the carpet. That was my dream, anyway.

That dream went up in smoke while we sat in Kristi's hospital room that night. The contractions got more intense and closer together. Stuff was getting real again, so we took a short walk to the elevator, went down to labor and delivery, and were immediately placed in a birthing room. No sound barrier, no hood-slide, no horn playing Dixie. Just a slow-motion, two-floor elevator ride. The whole get-it-done-in-forty-minutes theory was shot to hell as well. We were admitted to the hospital around nine-thirty Friday night. We didn't see a hair on that kid's head until a little after five on Saturday morning. All night long I sat there holding her hand, coaching her to breathe, watching the paper on the Richter Scale machine that charted the severity of the contractions get longer and filled with more ink every time one would hit.

By the time we got to the heavy pushing, Aunt Darla had joined us in the room. She worked at the hospital, so she was able to pull some strings to be in there. I'm not sure whether she was there to help Daphne or me, or both. No matter, I was just glad she was there. I was trying to be calm, cool, and collected for Daphne, but I was quickly turning into a bowl of jello.

When we got down to the severe pushing, my sense of humor had started to wear a little thin with the mother-to-be. *Charm, baby, charm* was no longer working. Once, in the middle of a particularly strong contraction, Daphne joined her family in wishing I had never been born. Everything went back to normal, though, as soon as she gave her last push, and our little surprise engagement gift to each other was in the hands of the doctor. I cut the umbilical cord and handed our perfect, little girl to her mother, and we were done. We had made a human being. We were parents. Our lives had changed entirely.

Hayley was a thousand pounds of joy in a six-pound package. She had her mother's eyes, dark black hair, and the skull of a conehead. It seemed she had gotten a bit sideways in the birth canal, and the doctor had to use forceps to assist the birth. In doing so, he made my little angel's head pointy. Every newborn baby looks like a lizard the first few seconds after arriving on the scene. Mine, however, was the prettiest little pointy-headed lizard that had ever been. I had a family of my own. At that moment, I was the richest man in the universe.

Newborn babies have a way of bridging gaps in families. Several months after we took her home, we were visiting Hayley's grandparents. After a particularly heavy meal of whatever strained veggies we were feeding her at the time, she put the load limit on the diaper she was wearing to the test. It was quick, it was vile, and it demanded to be dealt with.

Without a second thought, I jumped up, grabbed her and told Daphne I would handle this one. Honestly, it wasn't a big deal. We were a team. That sort of thing happened all the time. We thought that's what all parents did. As it turned out, we were wrong. When I brought Hayley and her freshly cleaned bottom back to the kitchen, Mrs. Davis met me in the hallway, looked me in the eye, and said the sweetest thing she had ever said to me. Come to think of it, it may have been the first nice thing she *ever* said to me. *Thank you for being a good husband and being so helpful to Daphne,* she said, gently putting her hand on my shoulder.

For more than twenty years after that moment, Mrs. Davis was in my corner. She became one of my biggest cheerleaders as well as one of my favorite people in the world. The best part was that once she signed off on me, most of the family fell in line. Even Uncle Rud, who had been forced to like me in secret, was able to end the façade. Mr. M.L. was the lone holdout. That man hated me. I didn't care. I was part of the family. Had I known all it took to solve my problem was a dirty diaper, I would have changed one of the other kids in the family before Hayley was even born.

Being parents seemed to come naturally to Daphne and me. We had it down to a science inside of a couple of weeks. We would sit around and talk about people we had known who had children and all their many complaints. We decided those people just weren't trying hard enough. *This is almost too easy* we would say to each other, as we lived in a bubble of dumbassery.

Hayley was the perfect baby. She slept all night from the day we brought her home. She rarely cried. She flipped her adorable little middle finger at all the horror stories we had heard about babies and the many ways they ruined your life. Even when she came down with colic, she was kind enough to experience her ninety minutes of screaming every afternoon from three-thirty until around five. During that time, she was in the care of my cousin Wanda, who watched Hayley while Daphne worked.

She was a joy to be around, and she was her mother's pride and joy. She owned me lock, stock, and barrel. I came home for lunch so I could help feed her. I rocked her to sleep almost every night. Once, when she was about three weeks old, I was feeding her, and I was trying to readjust her. For some reason, I decided to hold her bottle by the bottom with my teeth. When it inevitably dropped onto her face, it left a tiny, little scratch on her nose. She cried for forty seconds. I cried for the rest of the day.

The only thing about this child that wasn't wholly perfect was that she developed a hemangioma on top of her head. That's a harmless collection of blood that gathers under the skin, pools up and makes a red bump. It started tiny but ended up about the size of a quarter, and it stood up a full half-inch from her scalp. This made for some exciting photoshoots, as Daphne would try to cover it with hair, which never worked.

When it showed up, like all calm, collected parents, we completely freaked out. We made an appointment with Doctor Benak, and he assured us it was nothing to be concerned with. All we had to do was make sure she didn't bump it, and eventually, it would go away on its own.

As it began to grow, I quickly noticed something I would remember years later. People are rude as hell for no reason whatsoever. Total strangers would walk up to us in stores and parking lots, and without so much as a hello, they would start interrogating us about what was wrong with our poor baby's head. Without saying it out loud, they were adding, *and what did you do to cause this?* I began to make jokes about it, partly in hopes of making them understand it wasn't that big a deal, and partly to shame them. *We don't know what it is,* I would explain with a straight face. *All I know is that the doctor gave her to us at the hospital and told us under no circumstances were we to ever push the red button!*

One moment from Hayley's childhood that always brings a smile to my face is the incident at the county fair. We had taken her down to the fairgrounds for the evening to push her around in her stroller and get some outdoor time. As we casually strolled through the midway, no less than four strangers took time out of their busy night to inquire about the bump on Hayley's head, raising the temperature of my blood a little more with each question. I finally announced to Daphne I had had enough and was going to seriously embarrass the next person who dared broach the subject. Moments later, I would have my chance.

I saw her coming straight for us from across the way. I don't know how she even saw Hayley's head from her spot in line at the Deep-Fried Lard-On-A-Stick booth, but she did. (For clarity's sake, I should point out that I used Deep-Fried Lard-On-A-Stick purely as an example. I don't know what food she was buying, but we were at a county fair, so it's safe to assume it was both deep-fried AND on a stick).

As soon as she was close enough to make sure we were listening, her mouth opened, and the stupid fell right out. *What is wrong with this baby's head?* she asked, giving us a look that called our parenting skills into serious question. I paused for a moment for dramatic effect, looked at Daphne, then Hayley, then back at Lard Lady. I accentuated the drawl in my accent as much as possible and said *I'm not sure. She was doing fine until I put that cigarette out on her head a few minutes ago.* She stood there for a moment, looking into my eyes for a sign I was joking. Finding none, she spun on her heels and went to find the nearest police officer. The last time we saw her, she was disappearing into the crowd next to the Tilt-A-Whirl.

In future years, more people would say and ask even more outlandish things, but not about Hayley. They would be directed at our youngest son. By the Grace of God and with Daphne's help, I would eventually learn to handle the questions with a little more tact.

And so it came to pass that after three years of thinking we were the most exceptional parents in all of history, we decided to show the world how good we really were. We opted to have a second child. After all, we had done a remarkable job with Baby Number One, even with no experience. We couldn't even begin to imagine how easy another one would be. Cue the Heavenly laughter!

CHAPTER 11

MOVIN' ON UP – PART 1

L ife is about balance. Ask any parent, and they will tell you that no two kids are alike. If you are blessed with a calm, quiet, reserved firstborn, odds are that God will even things out by giving you a Tasmanian Devil in a diaper. We named our little devil Chandler, and he screamed his way into our world on June 4, 1996. That's the day he stole his mom's birthday. Having a baby on your birthday is the adult equivalent of having your birthday on Christmas. Both scenarios leave you with only two options: forget it or move it. Daphne has always been a trooper about it, though. She's always said Chandler was the best birthday present she ever received.

Chandler holds the record for the most expensive dinner I never bought. Around 6 P.M. that evening, Daphne and I were getting dressed for her annual birthday date night. I was in the bedroom putting on my boots when I heard her call my name. Once you've been married a few years, you learn to pick up on tone. There are many ways a wife can summon her husband.

Sometimes the tone is playful if you catch my drift, and you want to answer that call quickly. There's the *come in here and let me point out something you screwed up* tone, which the husband will respond to only after finding an excuse to avoid momentarily. If you've ever seen a man mowing his lawn in the rain, it's because he detected that tone. This time, Daphne said my name in the *get in here now this is not a drill* tone, and I knew something big was happening. My first thought was that for the first time in history, a woman had decided where she wanted to eat. Fat chance. She called me into the bathroom, where she was attempting to finish her makeup, to let me know dinner was off. That'll happen when a pregnant woman's water breaks.

Realizing that steak and lobster had just turned into ice chips and vending machine potato chips, I sprang into action. I took her arm and escorted her downstairs and into the car. Running back into the house, I retrieved our go-bag that had been waiting patiently by the door for several weeks. In what would become a lifelong trend, Chandler was overdue by a couple of weeks, and we were prepared for things to get crazy at any moment.

I threw the bag in the car, walked to the driver's side, and whispered a short prayer that all would be well with mother and child. Then I grinned like a jackass eating briars. I had been denied the opportunity of making the emergency drive to the hospital with Hayley. Not this time. This time I would become a combination of the Bandit, the Duke Boys, and Dom from *Fast and Furious*. It was the Granddaddy of Dad moments. My firstborn son was on the way, and I was about to drive it like I stole it to get his mom to the delivery room! He would be our first native-born Alabamian; the culmination of another of life's weird little journeys.

I didn't get serious about my career in radio until I was out of the business for a while. I had left the station in Ellisville after my first run-in with corporate radio. A company from Tennessee bought out our local owners, and for a while, things were great. They did a few things we all approved of, like pairing Cousin Ken with me on the afternoon show and replacing equipment that should have been replaced at least two decades prior.

We were living the dream for a while, but then they went and got all corporate on us. One day, out of nowhere, they announced that ninety percent of our staff was being fired, and they were moving the studios thirty miles down the road. I was one of a handful of employees offered a chance to remain. I believe this was the first time in my life I decided to make a stand. I was furious that hard-working people whom I considered friends were being shown the door so unceremoniously. I puffed up with righteous indignation and informed them I had no desire to work for a company that thought so little of its employees. I demanded that they reverse the firings, or they would have to limp along without me.

As I watched them limp away, I felt great about myself. I had stood up to the man. I was the hero of the working man. I would be remembered in songs and poems for years to come. I went toe-to-toe with corporate America and...and what?

Righteous indignation is a funny thing. You stand up for a bunch of people, lose your job defending their honor, and the ingrates don't even send you a thank you card! No songs. No poems. And worse yet, no paycheck. I learned a great deal that day. I'm still a massive pain in the ass to corporate America any chance I get, but with experience comes wisdom. I've learned to temper my propensity for fighting evil with a plan of some sort. Rule Number One: don't quit a job until you have another job. Once you know you have somewhere to fall, you can be as indignant as your little heart desires. That's important because Rule Number Two is: Righteous indignation doesn't feed the bulldog.

After showing the radio world a thing or two, I sought an opportunity to expand my horizons. I became the circulation manager of the *Laurel Leader-Call*, the local newspaper, fish wrapper, and birdcage liner in town. I spent eighteen months getting reamed by sweet, little old ladies who missed their paper delivery. If they weren't complaining about that, they were yelling at me because they found the paper next to the rhododendron plant instead of between the Jesus statue and the garden gnome. After that, I decided my horizons had been sufficiently expanded.

Radio gets in your blood. It's show business, even when it's on such a small scale as a radio station in Ellisville, Mississippi. I've always considered myself an entertainer, even as a kid. I don't know whether it stems from my childhood experiences, or if God put it there, but my heart has always had a hole that can only be filled by the affirmation of an audience. The size of the audience doesn't matter. It can be two people or twenty thousand. I NEED to perform for someone. It's who I *am*. That doesn't make sense to some people. Some might call it narcissism. I call it my life's mission. I firmly believe I was put on this Earth to entertain. That's why radio fits me like a glove. It's also why I missed it terribly. You don't get to perform much when you're out covering a paper route for a driver who called in sick for the third time in a week.

I had received word that there was an opening at WOKK in Meridian, Mississippi. So I made the sixty-mile drive for the interview and was hired on the spot as the new midday host. I bid a fond farewell to print media and returned to Country radio. The owner of WOKK, Mr. Eddie Holladay, was a self-made millionaire who had started work at his first station at the ripe, old age of fourteen. In the forty or so years since, he had built an impressive group of stations. He had expanded his empire to include signals in Mississippi, Louisiana, and Alabama.

A cantankerous, old fart with purple hair and a drinking problem, he was both friend and foe to me over the next fourteen years. After being on the air in Meridian for six months, he gave me my first morning show at WDJR in Dothan, Alabama, in 1994. It was just a few weeks after Hayley turned one. The catch was I also had to be the program director for the station. That way, we both got what we wanted; for me, an opportunity to finally see whether I had what it took to be the lead horse both on-air and off. For Mr. Holladay, it was all about filling two positions for the price of one. I didn't care. He gave me a shot, and I will be eternally grateful for the life he made possible by doing so.

We had been in Alabama two years the night Chandler was born. When I turned the ignition to head to the hospital, two thoughts rang through my head. The first was Daryl Waltrip, yelling *boogity boogity boogity boys, let's go racin'!* The second was the sobering thought that over the past few months we had spent more than our fair share of time in the very hospital we were moving toward.

I felt both lucky and blessed to even be alive for the upcoming festivities. Life has a way of throwing you a curveball when you least expect it. Earlier that year, our lives had ground to a paralyzing halt courtesy of my right testicle.

CHAPTER 12

OH, RIGHTY, WE HARDLY KNEW YE

Many dates are carved in granite in my life. The birthdays of Daphne and the kids, my anniversary, the days my parents passed away, the day I met Daphne, and February 15th, 1996. That's the morning I was awakened by the worst pain I've ever felt. It was a stabbing, constant pain in my extreme lower right side. The pain started about an hour before I usually woke up for work, so I didn't need the alarm clock.

Because I have a bit of a martyr complex, I decided I could handle whatever was going on, and I needed to get to the station. I don't know why I didn't take it as a sign of just how bad that idea was when I couldn't stand at first, and rolled out of bed onto the floor and literally crawled to the shower. After what seemed like an eternity, I managed to get to my feet, and ever-so-slowly made my way to the truck. I made it to the station, but the pain had become unbearable. I told my morning team they were on their own and went back home.

When Daphne woke up a little while later for work, she found me in a fetal position on the couch downstairs. By now, I had self-diagnosed myself based on the area of my pain. It was a kidney stone. It had to be. My Dad had suffered with them for years, and I had seen a stone smaller than the head of a pin reduce the strongest man I had ever known to a weeping heap on the floor. I had always feared they were inherited and had long suspected my time would eventually come. I was sure that was the day. The pain seemed to move lower into my extremities, thus confirming my diagnosis that the stone was on the move and I would soon pee it out and be on my way.

I tried desperately not to let Daphne know how bad I was hurting. She was five months pregnant with Chandler, and I didn't want to upset her in the least. She made me promise I would see a doctor, kissed me goodbye, and took Hayley to the daycare center at our church where Hayley played, and Daphne worked every day. As soon as I saw her leave the driveway, I dropped the façade and became a weeping heap on the couch. Like father, like son.

The pain subsided enough that I was able to catch a short nap while waiting for the doctor's office to open so I could call and beg for a same-day appointment. I woke up about an hour later and immediately knew something was wrong. The pain was now perfectly centered in my groin, and things didn't feel right at all. I decided to take a look, and to my horror discovered my right testicle had swollen to the size of a soccer ball. Okay, it wasn't that big, but it was every bit the size of a baseball. And the pain I had told myself two hours earlier couldn't get any worse, had doubled in intensity. I called my doctor, and they told me to get there as fast as possible.

The first thing my doctor did after looking at my mutant testicle, was to offer his opinion that I had a tortion. This is a condition in which a blood vessel that carries blood out of the testicle gets twisted, causing the blood to build up in the testis, which swells to insane sizes until...well, until. I didn't want to think about where the *until* part ended. He sent me straight to a urologist. If his diagnosis was correct, I would require emergency surgery to prevent *until*. I drove to the urologist's office, and sat there for three hours debating which of the two fates would be worse: death, or *until*?

I notified Daphne I might have to have surgery but told her to stay put until I knew for sure. I didn't want her to see me in the pasty-faced, cold sweat shape I was in as I tried to navigate the pain. They finally called me back for my exam. This would be the last moment I would see my dignity for several years. When a patient shows up at a urologist's office with a baseball-sized testicle, word spreads fast.

Soon my business was on full display for doctors, nurses, interns, assistants, and students. I'm pretty sure the janitor and two women from the lunch counter came by for a peek. Through it all, I just sat there, naked from the waist down, wishing giant, painful testicles on all of them, even the women. I know that makes no sense, but when you're in agony, you don't *want* to make sense. You want morphine.

After a thorough inspection of the area, tests were ordered. My situation had all the marks of the dreaded tortion, but we had to be sure. First up was a sonogram. I had seen quite a few sonograms during Daphne's pregnancies. Still, I was completely unaware that they made that equipment in a smaller size for looking into problems on men. As two male nurses entered the room and explained to me what was about to happen, I thought of my dignity sitting all alone in the waiting room. Was the pain really all that bad? Couldn't I just cowboy up and deal with it like a man? It would have to stop eventually, and there would be no need for all this fondling.

Of course, I knew better. I was going into hour nine of a level of pain I never dreamed existed, much less experienced. My ability to cowboy up had run out on the drive over. *It's just testicles*, I told myself. *They have them, too.* My first real indication that I might be in big trouble came when the nurse pulled back the sheet. He looked at my circus freak testicle, and said in the most sympathetic voice I had ever heard from a man, *I just want to cry for you, dude.*

Around five o'clock, nearly thirteen full hours after I crawled into the shower that morning, I sat on the butcher paper-covered table back in the exam room and waited. Much to my chagrin, when the doctor came in, he had more questions than answers. The good news—which turned out to be the bad news—was that I did not have a tortion, so *until* was not a threat. The bad news was, there was a mass inside my testicle. Unfortunately, the mass was surrounded by a massive infection. That infection was the source of both the pain and the swelling.

If you've never had a doctor look you in the eye and tell you that you have cancer, I'm not sure I can accurately describe what goes on in your mind. On this day, I would be educated on testicular cancer, the most common cancer among males between the ages of 18 and 34.

He talked for what seemed like an *eternity*. I didn't hear a word beyond *cancer*. My thoughts went immediately to the people waiting for me at home. My three-year-old, and my wife, who was 5 months pregnant with child number two. My boy. My firstborn son. Would I even be here for his birth? I thought about all the birthday parties, baseball games, dance recitals, and a thousand other memories yet to be made with them. I was twenty-six years old. I had never even entertained the thought of a life insurance policy. How would they survive? Where would they go? How was I going to tell Daphne she might be a widow soon?

Slow down, I told myself. *Listen to the man.* I forced myself back into the moment. He was explaining treatment options. With other forms of cancer, there are usually at least two plans. With testicular cancer, there is but one. The infected area must be removed. Hopefully, we had caught it before it got into my lymph nodes. It's aggressive cancer, and once it leaves the testicle, it spreads rapidly. That was the worst-case scenario.

And because cancer is the heartless bastard it is, we wouldn't be able to know what we were up against until we got rid of the infection. It was so thick and had so completely surrounded the mass that he couldn't be sure whether it was malignant, or if it had spread. I would have to go home with a massive dose of antibiotics and come back in two weeks for further tests. Two weeks. Fourteen days. Three hundred and thirty-six hours. An eternity.

At long last, fourteen hours after I completely missed the mark with my self-diagnosis, I was given something for the pain and embarked on the drive home. It was the longest ten miles of my life. During the ride, I made a decision that seemed like the right thing at the time. I decided to keep this information to myself. There was no need to drop this weight on Daphne's shoulders until the two weeks were up.

She was pregnant, and I had no idea what this kind of news would do to her. I told her about the infection but omitted everything he had said about cancer. I was terrified but determined not to let it show. I would make a few jokes, hold her tight, and give her two more weeks of cancer-free life. One of the things I loved about Daphne was how much she enjoyed being pregnant. I didn't have the heart to rob her of that joy. Not yet.

Time crawled. It's a cliché, I know, but it's also a truth. Knowing you have cancer is hard enough. Not knowing how bad exacerbates the issues in indescribable ways. I could hear the seconds ticking down in my mind, the space between each tick getting longer each time. It felt as though the two weeks before the next urology appointment was six months.

I was carrying on life as if the events of February 15th were a dream. I went back to work; I dove into my family life. As far as anyone—even those closest to me—knew, everything was normal. I spoke only to God about my unholy burden. Truthfully, it was more of a constant, whiny begging session than it was talking, but we were communicating.

I made plans to let Daphne in on the secret the day before the appointment. My original plan was to wait until I had the full diagnosis. However, the thought of her not being there holding my hand during what was sure to be the most awful discussion of my life was too much. I didn't just want her there. I *needed* her there. She was my rock, as much as I was hers. There was no way to do this without her. I was going to tell her at lunch. Then after work. Then during dinner. I finally mustered up the courage to tell her after we had gone to bed. I don't exactly know what I expected that conversation to be like.

Some twenty years later, I would learn the feeling of being on stage at a comedy club and telling a joke that laid down and died. That's reminiscent of the feeling I had when I told her this interesting, little piece of information. What the hell was I thinking? You can't look at your pregnant wife and say, *Well, goodnight, Sweetness. By the way, Doctor White told me two weeks ago that I have a tumor in my right testicle, and tomorrow we find out if it's killing me or not. Ain't that somethin'?*

Her reaction ran the full gamut of emotion. First and foremost, she was terrified. Running a close second, she was livid. She didn't understand how I could have kept something that big from her for so long. She didn't understand any of it. Nor did I. How could God do this to our family at such a crucial time? I've never been a big believer in the concept of life being *fair, but dammit, this isn't fair!* Why now? Why us? We wallowed in that for a minute, and then our spines stiffened.

We weren't ready to throw in the towel yet. We had a life to lead, kids to raise, and a future. We had dreams, and cancer was most certainly not one of them. We said a prayer and decided to hit whatever was waiting for us the next morning head-on. *We don't quit,* she said. It was not the last time she would pull me from the brink with those words. I held her tight as she gently cried herself to sleep.

I'm a comedian, by nature, and I try to find something funny in every situation. I hated to admit it to myself as I drove to Dr. White's office for the most important appointment of my life, but there was some funny in the lining of the cloud I was living under. My testicle had resumed its original size by then. The infection was cleared up, so the pain was gone. Not having to focus on white-hot searing death in my loins gave me the freedom to look at the lighter side of things. Of all things, why did it have to be testicular cancer? It was bad enough that half the employees of the hospital had taken a good, long look at my skipadeedoodah. Soon, I would have to tell everyone.

After this appointment, I would have to answer questions. Friends and family would want to know what was going on. Would they laugh out loud at the diagnosis or wait until I wasn't around? Then I had an epiphany: if you're going to have a disease, have a *funny* disease. If laughter is indeed the best medicine, something told me I was going to have a lifetime supply. My family has a wicked sense of humor, and don't even get me started on the people who work in radio. We are a strange lot, and no boundary has ever been found among us. Leave us alone long enough, and we will make some of the most offensive and inappropriate jokes imaginable. The subject of that dark humor would be me for a while.

Dr. White confirmed my fears when he told me the mass was indeed what we feared. The thing about testicular cancer is that you can't just open things up and take a peek. The tumor must be removed along with the testicle to be tested, which would take a week. You may have already figured out that you don't get your testicle back when it's over. To save your life, you must sacrifice one of the twins. Sometimes both. I was thankful I didn't fall into the second category. The surgery was scheduled for the next morning. There was no way of knowing what we were up against until the tumor was removed, and there was no time to waste. Aggressive cancer, remember?

Here's another cliché for you: That was the longest seven days of my life up to that point. My orders were not to return to work until after my next appointment with Dr. White. Two days later, I was in my chair in the studio hosting the morning show again. Daphne tried to talk me out of going back so soon. She quickly realized that just sitting around the house, going over worst-case scenarios in my mind, wasn't good for either of us. She finally relented and let me go.

I'm a sharer on the radio. I've always used real-life experiences as part of my show prep because my life is a subject I can speak about with great authority. I found early on in my career that listeners appreciate honesty. It brings them closer to you. Before they even realize it, they start caring about what's going on, and they want you to share more. So bright and early on a Thursday morning, I turned on the mic and laid it all out for them. When I said the word *testicular* on the air, my partner at the time, Roy Fox, nearly swallowed his tongue.

Roy was a great guy and an old-school radio dog who came up in a time where such words weren't spoken in polite company, much less on the radio. I figured I couldn't be the only one who had never heard of this cancer, and maybe spilling all the gory details during the morning drive would inspire someone to do a self-check. Perhaps I could be a small part of saving a life.

The good people of Dothan circled the wagons. The support was overwhelming. I had already been touched by the prayers and kindness of the members of First Baptist Headland, where we were members. For hundreds of total strangers to reach out was something I didn't expect. They vowed to be with me during the fight that lay ahead. With God, Daphne, and all these people in my corner, how could I possibly lose?

By dying, said the pessimist that lives in the basement of my mind. *You lose by dying.*

CHAPTER 13

AN AWESOME GOD

One man's medical oddity is another man's miracle. I learned that lesson when I went back for the seven-day check-up. I expected doom, despair, and chemotherapy on me. What I got was proof that God is still in the business of healing. I've never seen anything like it, Dr. White said with a bewildered look. A tumor is like any other organ in the human body. It needs blood to survive. The infection that nearly killed you two weeks ago was so thick that it choked off the blood supply to the tumor and killed it. Every single cancer cell inside that testicle was dead on arrival at the lab.

I am invincible. I am bulletproof. I am Superman. These were the thoughts of my ego in the first one-tenth of a second. Then, the practical side of my brain kicked in and said, *No stupid. God is invincible. God is bulletproof. God is Superman.*

Dr. White was rambling on about sending me to an oncologist just to be sure, but he didn't think any further treatment would be required. I barely heard him as I hugged Daphne so tight her eyes bulged. I was cured! I would be there for the birth of my son. I would get to teach him how to throw a football after all. There would be no widow in our house today!

The doc had already set up an appointment for me later that afternoon at the Oncology Center. Before I left, though, he wanted to have one more awkward conversation.

Who knew prosthetic testicles were a thing? I certainly didn't. He took me into a room where the displays were and gave me the option of choosing one if I wanted. Suddenly, I wished Daphne had waited outside. I don't know why it seemed so strange to me. If a man loses an arm or a leg, I assume there's a room to go in to check out replacements. Why should this be any different? I suppose it's because a man might decide he needs more than one arm or leg, and those replacements were at least functional. What in the world was I going to do with a plastic nut?

It took me about four seconds to decide against it. I had already experienced more embarrassment than a man should feel in a lifetime. I knew no matter what happened at the oncologist, there would be more naked-from-the-waist-down adventures at this hospital. And why not? Everyone there had already seen everything I had to offer. I politely declined and walked hurriedly to the car before they tried to sell me a sling or some weirdness like that.

I couldn't have imagined it, but the news got even better later that day. The oncologist had gone over my tests with a fine-tooth comb. He had determined I was cancer-free. He declared that he had never seen anything like it, the same as Dr. White. I told him I could sum it up for him in two words: *prayer works.*

He was prepared to put me on a chemo regimen if I wanted an insurance policy. Based on what the lab results showed, he gave me a ninety-five percent chance of having no further issues. Daphne and I talked it over for a few minutes and decided against any new treatment. If you gave me a hundred bucks and sent me to a casino with a ninety-five percent chance of winning, I would pounce on those odds like a cat on a limp-winged bird.

The trade-off was that I would agree to an ungodly amount of testing and follow-up appointments to make sure there was no resurgence of cancer cells. I accepted. Compared to the hellish list of things he guaranteed me I would experience with chemo, dropping my pants in front of strangers once a week for two years seemed like a bargain. Although I would revisit this decision a few times over the next year and wonder whether I had chosen wisely.

I've never seen any hard research on the average number of enemas a typical person has in a lifetime. Rest assured, I'm above average. I've had more dyes and meds pumped into my body from the wrong end I lost count. It seemed like every time I went in for an appointment, there was a scan that needed to be done that required the Roto-Rooter team to come in and torture me. Why is it that they tell you to let them know when you can't hold anymore, yet continue to pour it on when you do? I'm convinced some people only missed being a serial killer because they went to medical school. Why be on the run wreaking havoc on people when you can work in air-conditioned comfort and be paid for it?

The horrifying walk/run you do while trying desperately to batten down the hatches when they tell you that you can go "evacuate" became an Olympic-level event for me. I was tempted on more than one occasion to not make it on purpose. If there had been a shower close by, things would have been a lot different a couple of days. I tried to take it with a smile most days, but some days they just pissed me off. Once, they pumped me full of some chemical that made my skin turn blue. What the hell? I went back to work looking like a smurf. My boss made me go home. I didn't argue. Nobody takes you seriously when you're blue, anyway.

It was pure hell for the first year. Then the hell was reduced to six months. Then Three. Eventually, I made it to the seventh anniversary of the day I bid Righty a fond farewell. After giving my junk one final once-over, Dr. White smiled and pronounced me officially cancer-free. I had faced the beast, and victory was mine. We. Don't. Quit.

CHAPTER 14

CHANDLER, OLD JOE, AND GEORGE

I don't know why everyone in the state of Alabama decided to go for a leisurely drive that warm June evening, but there they were. I was in full NASCAR mode trying to get Daphne to the hospital, and they were out counting telephone poles. I managed to get our speed up to seventy once, but it only lasted for a mile or so. The best I could do was slam on the brakes a little too hard when we got to the door of the emergency room. It was not meant for me to make the stunt drive to the hospital for the birth of a child.

This was the night I found out how strong Daphne truly is. She's never been a fan of medicine. She doesn't like taking it, and she doesn't like being on it. She had kidney problems as a child and spent several years in and out of hospitals taking tons of meds, and that time left its mark on her.

On the night Chandler was born, she was doing her tough-girl routine, riding out the contractions. She planned to wait until the last possible minute before asking for the epidural. When the contractions began to get to a level she wasn't planning on dealing with, she requested the heaven-sent elixir that has made millions of deliveries easier for everybody. Unfortunately, by the time she asked, she was fully dilated, and the nurse told her it was too late.

My heart sank as I realized this woman was about to give birth the old-school way, with no pharmaceutical help whatsoever. Not so much as an aspirin. I shuddered to think about what she would soon be going through. I shuddered for me, too. I knew exactly who she was going to blame for the hell that was forthcoming. I told my knuckles it had been nice knowing them, and I squeezed her hand.

To this day, I have never been more in awe of another human than I was that night. I saw things that night I will never be able to unsee. Her body was doing things it was not designed to do. I mean, I suppose it was doing precisely what it was intended to do. But to me, it appeared as if the laws of physics were being broken.

I had taken a less-active role in Hayley's birth, choosing to stay close to Daphne at the top side of the stirrups. This time, fresh off a brush with death, I was determined to experience everything. I don't recommend it. There are some things a man just shouldn't witness. She was calm and collected, although in terrible pain. I was freaking out. At one point, I wondered whether they would give ME the epidural just so one of us could have some relief.

God's plan for reproduction is perfect. If he had put men in charge of the hard part, civilization would have died out with Cain. We would never have made it to Abel. The birthing process would be a one-and-done situation for a man. Women are stronger, gentlemen. Deal with it!

Jacob Chandler Broadway made his entrance (or exit, depending on how you look at it) just in time to say happy birthday to his mom. She didn't get that dinner I had planned, but she didn't seem to mind as she cradled her little man to her chest. We were now officially Broadway, Party of Four.

Chandler was a one-of-a-kind kid. He was the category five winds in the eyewall surrounding the blue sky and sunshine inside the eye of the storm that was Hayley. They were polar opposites, and they were the best of friends. She doted on her baby brother, and as they grew, they would put on concerts for Mom and Dad standing on top of a small picnic table in Hayley's bedroom. We played hide-and-seek every day for years. Chandler would never look under his bed, where I always hid, because he knew when he turned his back I would come out and tackle him, launching into a full-blown tickle attack. He was so much fun. He still is.

We shortened his name to Chan or Chan Man because we're Southern, and that's what we do. His first name, Jacob, is biblical, but his real namesake is Chandler Bing, from *Friends*. Could we *BE* any more cheesy?

Chan's legacy in our family, as far as I'm concerned, is that he completely mended the relationship between myself and Daphne's grandfather.

Chan had the most vivid imagination of any child I had ever known. He didn't have an imaginary friend.

He had an imaginary farm, complete with livestock, crops, and hired hands. His two trusted employees were a couple of old cowboys named George Strait and Old Joe. Old Joe oversaw the tractors and other implements required to run a farm located in the mind of a four-year-old. George Strait tended to the cattle, crops, and shopping. At night, he would sing to the cows. Chan would talk for hours about his farm. He painted pictures with his words that were so vivid you could hear the cattle lowing in the fields, as plain as you could see the tall grass behind the barn swaying in the wind.

One Sunday afternoon during a visit to Mississippi, when we were all hanging out in the kitchen at Daphne's grandparents, my boy launched into one of his prolonged dialogues about life on the Bar C Ranch. He was going into great detail about how the farm was located in the field behind Mom and Dad's house, giving his usual in-depth description of how it looked, smelled, and sounded. When he began to talk about George Strait and Old Joe, I noticed Mr. M.L. walk over to the bar next to where Chan was sitting and take a seat.

He was positively riveted by what he was hearing. He started asking questions. Chandler was more than happy to provide the answers. They spent the rest of the day talking about the farm. Before they were done, the impenetrable field of curmudgeonry that surrounded the old man had fallen like the walls of Jericho. They became best buds. I watched in amazement as this bitter, old man who had once thrown me out of his house for eating too many rolls turned into putty in the hands of my little storyteller.

At one point during the afternoon, he walked by me, gave me a big pat on the back, and said *that boy of yours is something else!* From that moment until the day he died, there was never another cross word between us. He finally accepted me into his watertight circle of family. One might go so far as to say we became friends. And I owe it all to a farm that didn't exist, constructed in the carefree mind of a little boy with big dreams and an even bigger imagination.

I love that boy, but he is his father's son. He is stubborn, opinionated, and has a lazy streak in him. However, put him to work, and he won't stop until the job is done. That's how I was raised, and that's how I raised him. Now, when I say 'work', I mean manual labor. Tell him to cut down a tree, and he'll do it with a butter knife. Tell him to clean his room, and he'll get to it eventually. Maybe.

I shared what little knowledge I have about playing guitar with him, and he ran with it. He passed me in guitar skills many years ago. He loves to perform. Singing, acting, playing drums or guitar, he does it all. He can't help it. He's a chip off the old block. He also has a knack for driving his mom to the brink of insanity. Again, that's an inherited trait.

The thing I am proudest of about Chandler is his heart. It's the size of Texas, and he's not afraid to let you see it. He is the kind of friend you want to have. He's the kind of brother a father wants for his children. He's the kind of son every father wants.

Now that he is all grown up, Chan is a man's man. Like his old man, he enjoys getting his hands dirty. He loves the outdoors. No animal with a legal hunting season attached to it is safe from him. He would rather hunt and fish than eat and breathe. I once saw him shoot a squirrel out of the top of a tree with a bow and arrow. Also, like his old man, he tends to temper his feats of greatness with moments of dimwittedness. Case in point: when he shot that squirrel, he took the bloody carcass into the house and started to skin it in the kitchen sink, which sent Daphne into cardiac arrest. It's a guy thing, I suppose. Adrenaline leads us to do amazing things but sometimes shuts down our ability to make good decisions.

Daphne and I have always been proud of the kind of little brother Chan is to Hayley. Still, the depth of his abilities would not be genuinely revealed until he became a *big* brother.

Brotherly love...

CHAPTER 15

MOTHER'S INTUITION

There's something wrong with this baby. Daphne made that announcement to me in hour two of labor for child number three. Her pregnancy with Grayson had been fraught with problems almost from the beginning. With Hayley and Chandler, she never had more than the usual issues every woman goes through when she is with child. Not this time. Almost immediately, she was plagued with sickness, unusual fatigue, and just general blah-ness in her daily life.

In the fifth month, she went for a regular check-up and got some news that was, to say the least, not good. She had developed a condition neither of us had ever heard of, gestational diabetes. This is a form of diabetes that plagues some pregnant women. It acts just like "regular" diabetes as far as what it does to the body, and if left unchecked can develop into full-blown Type 2 diabetes post-partum.

I had been present at nearly every appointment during all three pregnancies, but this day I had to be at a live broadcast and couldn't get out of it. When she pulled up at the location after the appointment, I could tell by her face something wasn't right. She tearfully explained what was going on, and what the treatment would be. We wouldn't know whether the diabetes was permanent until several months after Grayson arrived, and her body had returned to factory settings.

I consoled her the best I could, making sure she knew she was not in this alone. I hurriedly put on my brave face, the one I had used so frequently during my cancer episode. She gave me a half-smile when I told her everything was going to be okay, but something inside her said I was wrong. She would share with me years later that she couldn't put her finger on it, but she knew this diagnosis was just the beginning of something much worse and more far-reaching than even the doctors could predict.

When the contractions kicked in with Grayson, I didn't even attempt the breakneck drive. I picked up our go-bag, got her in the car, and we took off as though we were headed to Applebee's for dinner. I wasn't going to let myself be disappointed this time.

Not long after we were checked in, and all the monitors were hooked up and activated, an alarm started going off on the fetal heart monitor. If I had been attached to a heart monitor, it too would have sounded an alarm as my heart completely stopped working briefly. I looked at Daphne just in time to see the color drain from her face. This was our third time at-bat, and during the first two, not a single alarm sounded. When this one started screaming, it scared the hell out of us.

The nurse came in and explained that Grayson's heartbeat was not as fast or as stable as it should be. They would be monitoring the situation closely until he arrived. If his pulse sunk any lower, Daphne would need an emergency c-section. Neither of us wanted that, but it was a much better alternative than losing our baby. The nurse told us to keep Mom as comfortable and relaxed as possible. The epidural had already been put in place, so that wasn't going to be quite as hard as it sounded. A few minutes after the nurse left, Daphne looked at me with worried eyes and calmly said *there's something wrong with this baby.* She said it with such certainty I didn't bother trying to tell her she was wrong. Her eyes revealed hidden knowledge I didn't want to challenge.

Grayson picked a strange night to arrive. For some reason, the Labor and Delivery wing of the hospital just could not seem to get their act together. When we first arrived, we saw a doctor we had never seen. He explained to us that Daphne's usual OB was scheduled to cover the next shift, and they didn't call him in because she would be in labor long after the shift change. This poor shmuck was working with no less than five women, all in various stages of pushing, breathing, or taking their husband's names in vain. I'd never seen a headless chicken in scrubs, but there he was. He would pop into the room every forty-five minutes or so, take a look at the monitors and tell Daphne she was doing great. Then he would disappear again to repeat the same scene with another mom-to-be.

This caused quite the stir in our room when the contractions got serious. I called for the nurse, and she came in to check. She lifted the sheet, lowered her head for a peek, and when she raised her head back up, her entire face had disappeared behind the widest set of eyes I had ever seen. I couldn't tell whether the look was surprise, panic, or both. She took a breath, composed herself a bit, and said *I can see the head crowning!*

My response to this disturbing bit of news seemed obvious to me but appeared to take the nurse entirely by surprise. *Well, call the doctor,* I half-spoke and half-shouted. *This is why we pay him the big bucks!* That's the moment she dropped some knowledge that formerly had been held back. The doctor we didn't know who was making frequent cameo appearances, had delivered three babies since we arrived in the hospital. He was currently catching some z's in his office. And since we were now ten minutes past shift change, we would have to wait until our regular doctor appeared. She then said the damnedest thing I had ever heard. *I can't do this by myself, and this baby is coming. I need you to scrub up!*

The hell you say! Or something eloquent like that rolled out of my head. I was a thrice-trained Lamaze coach. My job was to encourage proper breathing. *I don't know nothin' 'bout birthin' babies,* I said, as I channeled Butterfly McQueen from *Gone With The Wind.* I was trying to be funny and not pee on myself at the same time. Nurse Stoneface wasn't in the mood for humor.

She sent me to the sink and told me to start scrubbing. Then she grabbed the gown that would typically go around the person getting PAID to do this sort of thing and told me to hold out my arms. She slid the gown over my arms and sent me to the foot of the bed.

Daphne was informing us both that she could no longer resist the urge to push, and that somebody had better get in position. I assumed my place behind home plate and prepared to catch Grayson. The nurse was literally tying the strings of the gown behind my back when the doctor burst into the room. He sent me back to the top of the bed where I not only belonged but desperately longed to be, crouched down, told Daphne to push, and lifted out the baby—a total of twenty-five seconds of work. I was thinking to myself how much it was going to suck if I had to pay this guy full price when I damn-near had to do his job, when his demeanor took a turn for the worse. Grayson wasn't breathing.

Oh my God, it's worse than even Daphne thought! was my initial reaction. Time froze. Daphne was asking what was going on. The doctor and Nurse Stoneface had our son on the table where a normal birth would see them cleaning up the little guy and getting ready to hand him to his mom. They were not concerned with cleaning. Grayson was aspirating. It appeared that during birth, his umbilical cord had experienced a tear. Because of his position in the birth canal, his airway had filled with bile, and who knows what else. He was drowning.

To their credit, they were very calm as they did their work, but there was evident concern on both their faces. It felt like an hour went by, but in reality, it was less than a minute before they cleared his airway, and the most beautiful cry we had ever heard filled the room. Despite the weak heartbeat and the aspiration, our little man was alive and well. We shed far more than a few tears as Daphne cradled him close and introduced herself.

For a fleeting moment, we were both convinced her early prediction had been nothing more than a bad case of nerves. It would be several months before we knew just how right she had been.

He's had that smile from the very beginning...

CHAPTER 16

A CONVERSATION WITH GOD

So there I stood, phone in hand. Doctor Benak had just delivered his eleven word bullets. I suppose when you ask your doctor whether your child is going to live or die, you should be thankful for *I don't know*. God knows it's better than a hard yes. At least with *I don't know*, there's a chance. I can say that now because I'm seventeen years past the question at the time of this writing.

At that moment, however, the two answers felt identical. How in the world, in the year 2003, could something be so rare that a pediatrician with more than thirty years experience had only seen it once? I was dazed. Confused. Crushed. Angry. Lost.

I held the phone in my hand for a couple minutes after the call ended. Part of me was hoping he would call back to let me know he had made a horrible mistake and mixed up his patient files. He would apologize profusely for giving me the wrong information. He would beg our forgiveness. When I realized how ridiculous that sounded, I hung up the phone and faced

Daphne. This was, and still is, the lowest point in our marriage. Neither of us had ever felt such hopelessness. We didn't know what to do. We didn't know what to say. We were both completely numb.

Tears were falling from her eyes, but she made absolutely no sound. The look on her face destroyed whatever pieces of my heart Doctor Benak had left intact with his call. I held her, and we wept. At that moment, Satan had planted his flag in our lives, and he was standing proud over us, waiting for us to turn our anger to God. For me, at least, he wouldn't have to wait long.

The silence in our room was broken by the phone ringing. It was Daphne's best friend, Judy, calling to see what we had learned about Grayson. I don't know why I even answered, but I did; when she asked about the test results, all I could get out was *we just got some really bad news*. I passed the phone to Daphne and left the room. I suddenly felt as if an elephant had perched itself on my chest. I needed air. I needed space. I needed to wake up from this nightmare.

As if the news itself had not been enough, and it most certainly had, it got worse. We got the call on Wednesday afternoon around four o'clock. Dr. B called back around four-thirty with the name and number of a pediatric neurologist at the Children's Hospital in Birmingham. I called immediately. The nice lady who answered let me know all the doctors were gone for the day, but I was welcome to call back the next morning between nine and ten, and I could speak to one of the specialists. I resisted the urge to beg her for a home number for one of them and returned to the pit of despair.

That night our home was filled with people from our church and our neighborhood. Word spread like wildfire in the little town where we lived, and everyone wanted to offer words of encouragement, prayer, and in keeping with the Baptist Crisis Handbook, pizza and casseroles.

Their presence was sweet, and while we were touched by their concern, deep down we just wanted them to leave.

The strangest thing about that night to me was that Grayson was asleep on a pallet on the living room floor. The room was filled with people at one point, but no one said a word. Everyone just stared at this helpless, little bundle sleeping so soundly and searched for words that couldn't be found. This situation was new for us all. As much as one might want to say *sorry about your kid's brain*, it's terrible form.

At one point, as we all sat and stared at Gray and wondered what was next, I heard our pastor who was seated on the couch next to me, gently say *bless his heart*. Those three words usually mean something else entirely in the South, but he said them in a broken voice that sounded much more like a prayer than a cliché. He was displaying a fantastic amount of empathy to our plight. He will never know what that meant to me, even though I've tried many times to explain it to him.

When everyone had gone home, Daphne went to bed. She was wiped out from the emotional drain of the day. I told her to go, and I would get Hayley and Chan to bed and make sure Grayson was tucked in. Half an hour later, I was the only one awake in the house, and I found myself standing over Grayson as he slept in his crib. I gently stroked his hair for a moment, and then—through another round of what seemed like an endless supply of tears—I had an honest conversation with God.

Not the kind of honest conversation where sins are confessed. That was a regular occurrence in my prayer life. No, this was different. It wasn't a prayer. It was a man-to-God talk in which I unloaded on him for allowing this to happen to my son. I was furious, and it was time I told Him so! I didn't even bother asking why. Why it happened didn't matter to me, just the fact that it did happen.

You know I'm not equipped to handle this, and yet you've thrown it on me anyway. What happened to you not giving me more than I can handle? I thought you knew everything. Unless you've turned a blind eye to me for the past ten years, you know damn well I can't handle this. I barely made it through cancer without having a breakdown, and now you give me this? What is wrong with you? Daphne was sick for the entire pregnancy, and we almost lost him in the delivery room. Wasn't that enough for you? What did I do to deserve the Job treatment? And what about Daphne? She's the greatest mom I've ever seen. She's doing such a great job with Hayley and Chandler, but now you're going to do this to her? How are we going to raise the older two when you've hobbled the youngest? What is WRONG with you? We try so hard to be good people. We go to church, we follow your rules, we give of ourselves. We do whatever we can to be salt and light in the world per your request. And this is your reward? Damn you!

Down the road, there would be a time when I felt even more separated from Him than I was at this moment, but until now, I had never felt so much space between us. And I wasn't done straightening Him out just yet.

Wait. I'm not done with you, God! What about Grayson? What kind of life have you stuck him with? After all that we've been through over the past year, are you just going to take him from us now? Is this your idea of a joke? If you were going to take him away from us, why didn't you just let us have a miscarriage? I know that would have sucked, but it can't be worse than having him here for less than six months just to watch him die from some rare disorder. I know this isn't just some freak genetic accident. This is your handiwork, and I resent you for it. I deserve better than this!

With that last piece of holy disrespect, the breakdown I had been avoiding since I found out I had cancer all those years ago came crashing down on me like a load of cinder blocks. After eight long years the weight of the world fell on me faster than darkness falls on a room when the switch is turned off. I leaned against Grayson's crib, trying to be quiet while several years of stress poured out of me like water from a jar. I could barely stand as I wept over my son. At that moment, he may as well have been in a coffin. I was mourning the loss of a person who was still alive.

You might not know this, but when you have an honest, open conversation with God, He will return the favor. You just need to listen. In the depths of my despair, He spoke to me. He accepted my list of grievances, and He offered a rebuttal.

Deserve? You're kidding me, right? If I gave you what you deserved, you'd be standing naked in a desert where the sun never sets with an empty canteen and no chance of rain! Why don't you get over yourself for two minutes and allow me to give you an explanation, which you ALSO don't deserve? You've got a lot of nerve, taking credit for getting through the cancer scare. Remember when you were going far and wide spreading the word about how I killed your tumor before the doctors even knew it was there? Remember how you called it a miracle? Where's your faith now? If I can cure you of cancer, what makes you think I can't get you through this? You and Daphne are about to endure some trying times, and if you stop trying to be a hero, I'm going to carry the both of you through it all.

And by the way, at what point did I say anywhere I would never give you more than you can handle? That's ridiculous! I give you more than you can handle all the time. Otherwise, what would you need me for? I'm going to allow you this moment, but as soon as you're done with your pity party, get off your ass and cowboy up. We have work to do. (This is a loose translation of what He said to me that night. He probably didn't say "get off your ass", but that's what I needed to hear, so that's what I'm going with. Don't judge me. God can say "ass" if he wants to. He's God.)

CHAPTER 17

PLAN THE WORK

At 7:30 the following morning, I was once again on the phone with the Children's Hospital in Birmingham. They told me to call at eight, but I was determined to be first in line. To my pleasant surprise, the pediatric neurologist we needed was available and ready to talk. Dr. Benak had sent Grayson's records, so he had already been briefed as to what we were up against. The first evidence that God was already at work came in the form of information. Sweet, blessed knowledge. The kind you get from a pediatric brain specialist who has seen the rare disorders you are calling about dozens of times throughout his career.

The first and most important subject was Grayson's chances of survival. The answer came in three words that completely erased the horror of Dr. Benak's *I don't know*. When he spoke them, I felt a warmth rising through my body as if I had been standing next to a fire. *One hundred percent.* He told me while it would be very challenging, Grayson should lead a long, healthy life.

I'm sorry, God. I should never have doubted you. It won't happen again. I'm officially off my ass. What do I do now?

We made an appointment to get Grayson to Birmingham as soon as possible, and with that, we took the first steps of a truly fantastic journey. In Birmingham, we would discuss the challenges Grayson would be facing, and the first members of an ever-evolving team would be assembled to get us on the right path.

After hanging up, I threw my arms around Daphne and held her so tight I'm pretty sure a blood vessel blew out somewhere. Like a football team down two touchdowns late in the fourth, we were behind on the scoreboard, but we could see the end zone. There was hope beyond the Red Zone, and it was time to activate our hurry-up offense and start a scoring drive. God had given us our son for the second time, and we were going to blow the darkness that had surrounded us so far straight to hell, and inject some sunshine into this boy's life. We couldn't expect Grayson to be a fighter if we didn't set an example for him.

We were Daphne and Jerry, the couple other couples professed to look up to as an example of what marriage should look like. We regularly received compliments from friends and family about the strength they saw in our relationship. Were we the super-strong partners they thought we were? As we held each other in the living room and shed tears of joy, we vowed to find out. We would solidify our marriage even more, stiffen our spines, and become what we never expected to be: the parents of a child with special needs.

We had no idea what we were walking into, and we didn't care. We didn't know what the doctor meant when he said Gray's life was going to be challenging. It didn't matter. Our prayer was that someone in this process knew what we needed to do, and we would follow instructions accordingly. This wasn't going to be easy. Then again, what good things in life are?

CHAPTER 18

WORK THE PLAN

Fast-forward through numerous brain scans, several dozen roadtrips to Birmingham, and a few drives down to Mobile to see the only pediatric geneticist in the state of Alabama, and you'll find Grayson's mom and dad sitting at the dining room table head-scratching while staring at a mountain of paperwork and pamphlets. We were several months removed from the initial consultation at The Children's Hospital and still didn't have an actual diagnosis. Frankly, his doctors were doing their fair share of head-scratching as well. Grayson, who was beginning a life-long trend of confounding even the most intelligent of specialists, didn't seem to fall into a specific category with his combination of issues.

We learned very early on that all doctors have one thing in common: they like to put things into a box because once you roll all the symptoms up into a ball and drop them into the right disease/condition box, you can then reach into the corresponding Treatment

Plan box and whip out a plan that may or may not be tried and true. Whether your particular box is cancer, arthritis, heart disease, or allergies, your doctor has the Treatment Box for you. That's not the case when you're missing one piece of your brain and have another piece that's too small, coupled with massive developmental delays and symptoms of autism.

That box is elusive. On more than one occasion, we thought we had it all figured out. Inevitably, some doctor would look into the box and say *Nope, he's missing seizures as a symptom.* Or they would tell us *he has everything but partial blindness,* or tremors, or a big toe where his pinky should be. It was enough to drive you crazy if you let it. We didn't.

Grayson's doctors were obsessed with putting a label on his situation. Subsequently, we became obsessed, as well. They convinced us that if we just had the right box, the perfect plan could be put into place to get him started on the proper regimen of therapies and, if needed, meds. We pored over medical journals and what little assistance we could get from the Internet in 2003, trying to rush a diagnosis. We were ready to get to work. Grayson was already receiving physical, occupational, and speech therapy several times weekly, but even his therapists were confused about what they should be doing due to lack of a diagnosis.

This rocked on for months until the day we made our last trip to the geneticist in Mobile. He was a Latin-American with a name I couldn't even begin to pronounce, so I quite politically incorrectly referred to him as Ricky Ricardo. Not because of stereotypes, but because when he spoke, his voice sounded exactly like

Lucy's hapless husband to me. Every time he opened the door to the exam room, I half-expected to him yell *Graaayson, I'm hooooome!* He was an incredibly nice man who seemed to genuinely care about Gray, and ultimately the chore of deciding which box was for Grayson fell squarely on his shoulders. He went down the list of genetic disorders each time we had an appointment and would eliminate suspects one-by-one. He was fond of a condition known as Angelman Syndrome. He kept coming back to it time and again, but there would always be one or two symptoms missing. The symptoms are:

1. Microcephaly (abnormal development of the brain resulting in a smaller-than-usual head)
2. Intellectual or learning disabilities
3. Developmental delays
4. Short attention span
5. Ataxia (a lack of voluntary muscle coordination, which causes problems with walking, speech, and eye movements)
6. Strabismus (both eyes don't align properly when looking at an object, causing issues with depth perception)
7. Seizures
8. Speech impairment
9. Aggressive behavior (in 7 out of 10 patients)
10. Hypotonia (poor muscle tone) with hypertonia of limbs (muscles in legs and arms are stiff, almost rigid sometimes)

From that list, Grayson exhibited everything except seizures and aggressive behavior. That didn't mean anything really, because these often don't show up in the Angelman Syndrome child until they get a little older. Dr. Ricardo liked this diagnosis for Gray, but he never committed to it wholly, because seizures had accompanied the other symptoms in almost all of the Angelman patients he had dealt with.

We had made the four-hour one-way drive to his office several times during the previous months, and I was getting a little frazzled about what seemed to be wasted time. I didn't blame Dr. Ricardo. It certainly wasn't his fault. It just seemed like we were throwing good money after bad trying to find a name for this that may never be found. Daphne and I had already been having that conversation, but this would be the day I decided enough was enough. Why did it need a name? What would that do other than help the doctors make sense of something they couldn't make sense of? We bid the good doctor a fond farewell and set out for the journey home.

On that ride, we had a long talk about doctors and treatments and therapists and plans. Mostly though, we talked about Gray. That little man in the back seat, taking up barely a third of the space provided by his car seat, deserved better than he was getting. We agreed we had fallen down a rabbit hole. We, along with the doctors, were doing nothing more than trying to make ourselves feel like we had accomplished something by finding *precisely* the right diagnosis. Meanwhile, Grayson was losing valuable time when we should be doing anything and everything that could be done to help him.

We returned home with a new plan. We would tell the doctors we no longer cared about a diagnosis. We cared about Grayson and his needs. They could call it The Hippy Dippy Clown Disease for all we cared. It was time to roll up our sleeves and get to work. Forget drilling down to the precise plan they thought we needed. We instructed all of them, via Dr. Benak, that effective immediately, we would be painting in broad strokes. No more discussion of what Gray would never be able to do. We would figure that stuff out in due time.

For now, we wanted his therapists and doctors to treat him as though anything was possible. We didn't want *targeted* therapy and treatment for him. We wanted the works. As for the Box of Conditions, they were welcome to work on that in their own time and get back to us when they figured something out. We had already been told that from a health standpoint Grayson was fit as a fiddle. He had no life-threatening health issues, so we felt good about focusing on whipping his little body into shape. We wanted to give him a chance at doing whatever he put his mind to.

Let me tell you, they obliged. Susan, his first physical therapist—who quickly became a family friend—led the way. Three times a week, she would come and sit on the floor with Gray doing mundane things like letting him grip her fingers for as long as he could, and picking up his legs to help him stretch those rigid muscles. The occupational and speech therapists fell right in line as well. At last, we were getting some work done.

When you have a child with a limited understanding of what his limbs are for, it's a slow, grueling process to teach him how to use them. Weeks would go by with little or no improvement, and then we would see a glimmer of hope. Acts as simple as picking up a rattle and shaking it intentionally became moments of grand celebration. We cheered and clapped and woo-hooed a lot in our house back then. We still do.

One of the most significant issues we struggled with early on was getting him to sit up on his own. Like all babies, you could pick Gray up and pretty much do whatever you wanted with him. Put him on his back. Lay him on his stomach. Hold him on his belly in your hands and pretend he was flying. That last one wasn't part of his therapy, I just thought it was fun. His mile-wide toothless little grin told me he agreed. After six months of nine therapy sessions per week, we had gained the total of no ground in the sitting-up department. That's when Susan recommended we give hippotherapy a try.

My first response was about as dumb as you might expect. *What the hell can a hippopotamus do for him?* Susan flashed a wry, little smile that said this was not the first time she had encountered ignorance on this subject. She explained that hippotherapy is the use of horses in therapy with kids like Gray. Sitting up on a horse uses every muscle in the body. It strengthens the all-important trunk muscles that enable you to hold yourself upright. We decided to give it a shot.

I've been asked many times about the effectiveness of hippotherapy. I've given talks on the subject to civic groups. I will champion this form of therapy until my dying day. We took Grayson to the ranch for his first session and watched in real-time as a miracle happened.

I don't know what it is about horses, but they have this beautiful spirit about them that seems to know someone special is getting into the saddle. Twelve hundred pounds of muscle that could quickly kill a full-grown man turns to putty in the presence of a child with special needs. Don't ask me to explain it. God made horses, not me. I just know that it happens.

Grayson was cute personified in his riding helmet, which was too big for his little noggin. When they put him in the saddle, he just slumped over the same as when we tried to get him to sit anywhere. The therapist patiently led him around the arena for the half-hour session. It was evident that he was completely worn out when it was over. When we got him home, Daphne wanted to give him a bath because she's a germaphobe, and her baby boy had been touching an animal for thirty minutes. She put him in the apparatus we had in the tub to help him sit up.

Suddenly, this boy who had been incapable of sitting up on his own due to a lack of strength and understanding of how to use his abdominal muscles....sat up. One thirty-minute session had done what six months of therapy could not. It was nothing short of amazing. Grayson spent several years in hippotherapy and still loves riding horses to this day.

We were making progress, and it felt great. We had thrown ourselves into his therapy, and we were determined to give him the chance to do everything the doctors said he would probably never be able to do. Things like walking, talking, feeding himself, and being able to play in the backyard like other kids. We talked to him every day and told him how strong he was, how

133

great he was doing, and what an amazing kid he was. Everything was going great. Or so we thought.

CHAPTER 19

THE DEVIL IN THE FRONT OFFICE

Hello. My name is Jerry, and I'm a workaholic, and I come from a long line of the same. I was raised under the belief that if there is work to be done, do it. Forget how long it takes. That's not important. The only thing that matters is that at the end of the day, there's nothing left to do, whether it takes eight hours or eighteen. That's how I spent many of the earlier years of my career.

My staff at the radio station regarded me as a machine, and they would do pretty much anything for me. I was that boss that would never ask you to do anything I wouldn't do myself, and I proved it regularly. I gave my heart and soul to that station and its parent company for twelve years before Grayson came along. Then my priorities changed. Unfortunately, for me, I had set a precedent that would prove to be impossible to maintain.

When Grayson was first diagnosed, I was a wreck. There wasn't a snowball's chance in hell I could go on air for my morning show and be funny or entertaining. All I could be was a wreck. My boss at the time seemed to have an unusual moment of apathy and told me to take all the time I needed to sort things out. That was great because we had all those trips to Birmingham and Mobile to make, and at the time, we had no idea what was about to happen. He actually seemed to care when he called to tell me. I should have known better, but I was in such a broken state emotionally, I didn't bother to think about who I was talking to.

Because he's an attorney that hates me, and I'm allergic to lawsuits, I will protect his identity. Let's just call him Mr. Cypher. Mr. Lou Cypher.

Here's who I was talking to: A man with anger management problems who once picked a fight with a co-worker and fired him. Hours later, he hired the guy back. The stipulation for the rehire was that the *co-worker* attend anger management classes. A man who forced another co-worker to lie on-air about giving away a thousand dollars to the ninth caller because he didn't want to take the prize money out of the prize money budget. He made the poor guy manufacture a name to congratulate so it would sound like we did the contest. In a drunken rage, he once hit his ex-wife with his car and had to be bailed out of jail by his overnight DJ. He was as close to pure evil as I've ever encountered. Someday he will be the star of another book I'm going to write about my adventures in radio. For now, suffice it to say that he was a fourth-degree jackass.

This would be the first hard lesson I learned about the world as a special needs parent, and it was a big one. It would be so beautiful if the rest of the world could see what you see, feel what you feel, endure what you endure. If they could, they would understand, and they would cut you some slack when things take a hard left in your life. It would also be nice if Democrats and Republicans would work together for the betterment of our country, if it was sunny and eighty every day of the year, and if carbs didn't contain any carbs. None of those things are going to happen.

Through the years, I've had the opportunity to talk to parents who found out their unborn child was going to have issues. I always caution them not to look at the world through rose-colored glasses. People will *ooh* and *aah* when they see your adorable, new baby. They will put their hands on your shoulder and tell you how strong you are. They will offer their prayers, and in some cases, their assistance. Then they will return to their unchanged lives and expect you to do the same.

Obviously, this doesn't apply to everyone. There are some exceptionally wonderful people in this world, and they seem to show up at just the right time. Unfortunately, they are the minority. Mr. Cypher was not one of these people.

Take all the time you need lasted six days. On day six, Mr. Cypher had my morning show partner call and tell me if I wasn't back on the air the next morning, there was no need for me to ever come back. He was also kind enough to point out since my son was having *all these problems,* it would behoove me to be there, so I didn't lose my health insurance.

It was the first of many times he would hang that damned insurance over my head. He wielded it like a weapon, and any time he wanted to force my hand, he used it ferociously. Sadly, I wasn't as strong then as I am now. The thought of losing that insurance terrified me. So bright and early the next morning, I was back on the air.

I did confront him about threatening to fire me after he told me to take time off, and he promptly denied it. I took him at his word this time, but he would prove time and again over the next few years that his denial was as empty as his heart. But it wasn't just Mr. Cypher who resented New Jerry and his new set of priorities. Some members of my dedicated staff, who sang praises to my name when I was in the building sixteen hours a day for years, turned on me as well. It just took a little longer for them.

In retrospect, I suppose I didn't make it easy on anybody. When Grayson began his therapy regimen, I vowed to be at every session, or at least most of them. I adjusted my work schedule in such a way that I could do the morning show, leave the station around ten-thirty a.m., and go home. All of Gray's early intervention therapists came to our house to work with him, and we scheduled them all in the middle of the day. I would get home, eat a quick bite, and wait for therapy to get underway. Around three o'clock, Hayley and Chandler would get home from school, and I would spend a few minutes with them before heading back to the office. Once there, I would finish anything that needed to be done, no matter how long it took.

Most all the duties of my job as Program Director and Operations Manager of the building were in preparation for the next day. If I needed to have a meeting with a co-worker or a client, I scheduled it in the afternoon. The building would clear out at five, and I would stay for several hours wrapping up my day. It seemed like I had a sound system in place. I was thankful to have a job that afforded me that kind of flexibility. Everything that needed doing was getting done. I felt like I had the best of both worlds. The next summer, the revolt happened, and all that changed.

As much as I appreciated the schedule I had worked out, it was taking its toll on me. I was always in motion, running from home to work, back home and back to work, sometimes two or three times a day. In a small-market radio station, there's no such thing as a weekend. Even when I didn't have the office work and the therapy schedule, I was somewhere standing in a parking lot trying to sell cars or mattresses, or God knows what else. I was tired, but I was hanging in there. Grayson was worth it.

One thing you should know about radio: it's shark-infested waters, especially in the smaller markets. You may be the king of the mountain, but there is always someone gunning for your job. And while I refuse to lump all radio people into the same category, radio has more than its fair share of narcissists. Ego is a necessity to do what we do. Don't ever believe someone on any level of show business who says they don't have one. It's a lie. We all do. We feed off the affirmation of the crowd. We love the sound of applause. It feels great when the person working the drive-thru window recognizes your voice when you order. That's ego. We all have one, but not all are created equal. In radio, there are those with an insatiable desire for power. These are the ones you have to watch out for because when they mix that power with their overactive ego, they will inevitably abuse it. Mr. Cypher is a great example.

And so it came to pass that in the spring of 2004, one of the bigger egos on my staff decided it wasn't fair that I should get to work a split day if he couldn't. I don't know why it mattered to him, but it did. And he made enough noise about it among the staff that he eventually convinced some of them that he was right. Something had to be done. They decided to wait until the time was right, and then they would strike. They didn't have to wait long. Mr. Cypher, who knew full well what I was doing every day (mainly because he approved the plan before I implemented it), apparently had one too many martinis for lunch and came back to the station to have a talk with me about something.

Because it was early in the afternoon, I wasn't there. As was his tradition, his head exploded. Never mind making a call to let me know I needed to come back for whatever emergency he had cooked up over his booze-soaked vegan lunch. That would be too easy, and easy just wasn't his style. He called every member of my staff into his office one-by-one and canvassed them about my excessive absences *during the most crucial part of the day*, which, of course, was whatever time Mr. Cypher needed to see you.

That afternoon I received an email concerning an air staff meeting the next morning. I found that a bit odd, because the only person who ever called air staff meetings was yours truly. It was less of a meeting and more of a celebration of Festivus, the made-up holiday created by George Costanza's dad on the show *Seinfeld*. Part of the Festivus celebration was known as the *Airing of Grievances.* That's what was happening in the conference room that day. The air staff from all three stations under my charge were gathered for the ambush.

Mr. Cypher came into the room, his face already beet red from whatever elixir he was filling his coffee mug with. He informed me that everyone in the room had come to him at one time or another over the past year concerned about the fact that I was never in the building when someone needed me. Then he opened the floor so that these people, most of whom I considered personal friends, could let me have it. It was easy to pick out the small group that had been waiting for this moment. They pounced first, and they pounced vigorously. Anytime they needed me, I was gone.

Salespeople had asked about me once or twice in the middle of the day and had to be told I was gone. I was never in the station. They felt like they had no leader. They were adrift in the ocean with no rudder. That sounds ridiculous, I know, but they were bringing their drama A-Game to the table.

I listened intently. The mutineers had their say, and then Mr. Cypher went around the table asking everyone to dump on me individually. More than half of them had nothing to say, and you could almost see the fear in their eyes as they disappointed Lou by not coming through for him. When they were done, I sat there, stunned for a moment, and let it all sink in. I resisted the urge to pick up my chair and throw it at Cypher, gathered my thoughts, looked each of them in the eye, and said my piece.

I have been a part of this company since 1994. That's ten years. I've watched us go from one station in that little rat-hole building down the street with the leaky roof to a three-station cluster in a beautiful, new facility. The Country station, which you all know is my baby, has been the number one station in this market for seven straight years. I'm not taking credit for that, but I'm proud to say I'm part of that success. We have overcome so many things through the years as a team, and that's what we are; a team. Most of you were here when Grayson was born. Most of you have been to my home for staff parties or just to hang out, and you've met him. You know what I'm up against.

Yes, my schedule has been a bit odd for the past year, but that was never meant to last forever. I've never failed to come back and take care of whatever you need from me since all this started. No one has said a word to me about any of this until now. I'm disappointed you didn't think you could trust me enough to talk to me. You know I have an open-door policy and always have. Beyond that, let's talk about my priorities. They're different now. Radio is very important to me, but it's not even in the same zip code of importance as Grayson. This kid is struggling to do simple things that every one of us at this table takes for granted. But because of my schedule, I've been able to be there to see him make accomplishments. I was there when he held his bottle for the first time without help. I saw him sit up on the floor during therapy with no assistance for the first time. These are important things in my life now.

My two older kids didn't get all the attention they deserved from me the past few years because of this job. I'm not going to make that mistake with Gray. Put yourself in my shoes for a minute: If you were me, where would you rather be when Grayson takes that first step the doctors say he may never take? By his side, or here at this table? I'm not sure what you thought we were going to accomplish here today. I assume when this is *over, I'm going to get a mandated schedule that won't allow me to leave work for therapy anymore. If that was your goal, congratulations. But I want you to think about the things I'm being pulled away from, so I can be here to hold your hands while you do a job I long ago trained you to do. Now, if there's nothing else, I'm going to my office to get some work done.*

And with that, I left the table and went to my desk. It wasn't quite as dramatic as I would have liked because the conference room was literally outside my office door. I only had to walk about ten feet to the door, but I did slam it when I went inside, so there's that.

I sat at my desk and looked at the time. I noted in my head that the clock of my career had just been converted to a timer, and it was running backward. It was just a matter of time before the hammer would drop, and my insurance would be gone. I felt my stomach knot up when I realized the only thing saving me at that time was the fact that my station was number one. If those ratings dipped, even a little bit, Lou Cypher would seize the opportunity to blow me out of the building. He didn't like me. He had never liked me. He wanted a yes man. I didn't have it in me not to question things that needed to be challenged.

Unfortunately, Mr. Cypher had won, whether I wanted to admit it or not. My little speech meant nothing in the grand scheme of things. Sitting at that desk fuming, I allowed fear to creep into my life again. I couldn't lose this job. I would have to change my priorities again. As important as it was for me to be there for Gray, he needed me to keep this job. We needed that insurance. I needed to know he was getting the best care available, and without that insurance, there was no chance of that.

Something broke inside me that day. I didn't even realize at the time, but when I slammed that office door, I took the first step down a hill that would carry me to the darkest place I had ever been. Before I was done, I would lose everything I cared about.

CHAPTER 20

WHEN IT ALL GOES SOUTH

U p until now, you've probably been under the impression that I'm a pretty good guy, and until you get to this chapter of my life, I'd like to think you are right. Unfortunately, even the best guys can fall, and as Hank Williams once said, *When I fell, the whole world must have jarred.* Odds are by the time you're done with this chapter, you're not going to like me very much. Hell, just writing it down makes *me* not like me very much. You should look at this as a cautionary tale of how fear opens doors in your soul that are so secret even you don't realize they are open, and nothing good ever walks through those doors.

Fear does things to a man, and Mr. Cypher made sure I lived in a constant state of being afraid of losing my job and my insurance. He reminded me frequently of how great the coverage was, and how expensive COBRA coverage would be. He planted seeds whenever he could about how hard it would be to get Grayson covered with his myriad of pre-existing conditions. Once he knew there was a button to push to get me in line, he pushed it often and with sadistic glee. I let him get inside my head, and then all hell broke loose.

I'm not going to let Cypher take all the blame for what happened. Decisions had to be made, and I made them. I could have stopped my downhill slide at any point. Unfortunately, I was suffering from a severe case of cranial-rectal insertion, which clouds one's decision-making skills.

For the past year-and-a-half, I had slowly devolved back into my workaholic ways. I was determined to keep my job, so I wouldn't have to worry about Grayson's medical care. Keeping the job became an obsession. I knew I was good enough to keep the station at the top of the ratings food chain. If I had to miss a few therapy sessions and doctors' appointments here and there, everyone would just have to understand. I was doing it for the greater good.

Somewhere along the way, I convinced myself I was a hero for making this great sacrifice. I became *too big for my britches*, as my mom used to say. I began to build a wall around myself to keep everyone out. I no longer trusted my staff after the great Conference Room Revolt. I became suspicious of their every move. I was becoming an ass, and the only person who didn't see the transformation taking place was me.

If my troubles had stayed at work, things might have worked out differently, but once those secret doors open, the devil walks right in. The Bible says that we all have an enemy (Satan) who seeks to steal, kill, and destroy us. I knew the verse well, but I didn't understand the nuances of how subtle he can be. He whispers in your ear that everyone is out to get you. He convinces you that you are underappreciated and no one understands you. Then, when you're at your weakest, he deploys his biggest weapon. He speaks directly to your ego, telling you that you deserve better than what you have. When you start listening to that message, you're screwed.

As you might well imagine, being the mother of a special needs child is challenging. It's also exhausting. You find out very quickly who your real friends are. Those who genuinely care for you will accept your crazy schedule and understand the difficulties. Those who were just hanging around for a good time disappear almost immediately. They are terrified of what they don't understand, so they find reasons not to come around anymore until you finally stop asking them. Rest assured the number of friends that stay is vastly smaller than those who don't.

That was Daphne's life at the time. A small number of friends, and a husband who had gone from being a dependable partner to a guy who could only be counted on to be there occasionally. I had work to do. She would just have to manage Grayson on her own. I was the great American hero, Insurance Man, and my duties at work were far superior to anything she needed me for at home.

When a couple marries, each one brings a fair amount of baggage into the relationship. Some of it is good, some is bad, but it all comes along for the ride. The goal is to put all that baggage into a pile and unpack it together. That way, when you create your own baggage together, you'll at least understand where your partner is coming from. As happy as we had been in our marriage, Daphne and I never unpacked our bags. We were fourteen years into our marriage, and we were about to find out that we hardly knew each other.

Daphne's most prominent issue in her life was that her father abandoned her family when she was barely four years old. He walked out, divorced her mom, got remarried, and washed his hands of Daphne and her sister. He would occasionally send a birthday card, but he offered no financial, and worse, no emotional support whatsoever. I can't imagine what it was like for her as a child to feel like she was regarded as a mistake. She grew up with massive abandonment issues. She had muscled her way through those feelings when I was working sixteen hours a day before Grayson, but she was struggling now. To her, it felt like I was turning into her father and shirking my responsibilities.

And then there was me. I grew up dirt poor, with a dad who worked like a robot trying to make ends meet, only to come home from work one day and find out his wife had forsaken him because she had grown tired of their way of life. Questioning my dedication to my job was a personal insult to me, and I didn't take it lightly.

When you pour the contents of those two bags into a single pile, you get a dumpster fire. And once again, there was no water in the pumper truck. I felt like I needed to be gone all the time to save the insurance to prove my love and dedication. She needed me to be present in our marriage. Daphne has two love languages; spending time together, and acts of service. I was speaking neither. She became angry, then bitter. I responded in kind. It started small, and then it consumed us. And through it all, the voice in my head kept repeating *you deserve better than this!*

I won't bore you with the details, but the fights became longer, louder, and more frequent. The voice kept whispering. When I sought advice from people I thought were my friends, they only added fuel to the fire. *No marriage is strong enough to survive the stress of a handicapped kid.* I wish I had a nickel for every time someone floated that crappy advice my way. And they always said it with great certainty and authority, as if God sends kids with disabilities into a marriage as a form of punishment. The voice would agree wholeheartedly. I absorbed enough negativity to kill the vibe at Disney World. Worse yet, I started to buy into it.

One night, in the middle of a nasty argument, the voice reminded me of what I deserved. There had to be more to life than this constant bickering every time I came home. We had reached the point where we could barely say hello to one another without a fight breaking out. We were both nearing the end of our ropes. I decided to let go. I walked out of the house, leaving the girl of my dreams on her knees sobbing uncontrollably, lamenting that her babies were going to grow up without a Daddy as she did. I'm ashamed to say I remember thinking *I never realized how weak she is.*

If you're thinking I'm a horrible human being, hold on. I had not even begun to reach the bottom of my barrel of wretchedness. It gets worse. *So much worse.*

I drove around for a couple of hours that night, trying to determine my next move. I had spent years building the brand of Jerry Broadway on the radio. On the air, I was Superman. I was the ultimate family man, a hardworker, a good Christian, and I participated in every charity event I could find for more than a decade. I was loved and admired all over town. If word got out I abandoned my family, it would be devastating to the brand. We can't have that, can we? Then I came up with a plan that could only have derived from the depths of hell. If I couldn't divorce her, I would make her divorce me. That way, she's the bad guy, and I'm the victim. Marriage wrecked, brand saved.

I went back home, gave her a big hug, and told her I was sorry. The wrong kind of sorry. The type of sorry with a *but* attached to it. *I'm sorry, but if this happens again, I'm gone.* So much for charm, baby, charm.

CHAPTER 21

PORTRAIT OF A MIDLIFE CRISIS

To paraphrase a well-worn quote from John Wayne, marriage is hard. It's even harder when you're stupid. Welcome to my year of stupidity. What makes a man stray from his marriage? Stress, loneliness, financial woes, infidelity, the list is practically endless. With me, it was more profound than any of that. I found myself, through my inaction, with a massive void in my soul where God used to be. Somewhere in the mess that had been my life over the past eighteen months, I stopped going to church. Then I stopped spending time with my friends who still gathered in fellowship every week. At one time, I was surrounded entirely by rock-solid believers who enjoyed every minute of their lives, but still gave their lives to Christ.

Once I started listening to that voice, I didn't feel comfortable in their presence. I wasn't in the mood to think about others or spend time talking to people who didn't walk the path I was headed down. The *self* path. That path promised all the good things I thought I deserved, even though I had to step over a pile of broken hearts to get to the end.

I had discarded my compass, and I was drifting further and further from anyone who cared about me, and worse, God Himself. When I could no longer see any of them, it was just a matter of time before I went off the rails.

If you're married, don't fool yourself into thinking the only way you would ever break your vows would be with some supermodel you bump into at the grocery store. More often than not, it's just a regular person in your life who says or does something at the right time, and it gets your attention. If you're having trouble at home, something as simple as a friendly conversation with a co-worker can lead to so much more. She's easy to talk to. She listens to your troubles and offers advice that feels wise. Suddenly you're spilling your guts to someone who may be adrift just like you, and those conversations get more prolonged and more in-depth. Before you know it, you kiss her just to see if you can. Then you convince yourself you are no longer in love with your wife, and it's time to cut ties with a life you've spent years building.

The next step is getting tangled in a web of lies and deceit that erases every shred of decency you thought you possessed. Suddenly, you find yourself living in a hotel waiting for your wife to file for divorce because you don't have the balls to do it yourself. After all, you have a brand to protect. I know what I'm talking about. That's exactly how it happened to me.

As if it weren't bad enough that I had left Daphne to handle raising three kids, one with a massive handicap, the co-worker was also married. I was so wrapped up in self-pity it didn't bother me for a second that I was destroying not one, but two, marriages. She was having trouble at home, too, and decided being with me was a much better plan for her. What she didn't know was that I had no intention of having a life with her. She was a means to an end. I needed Daphne to hate me enough to pull the trigger on divorce. Once she filed, I could be the victim, and all would be well. My deranged mind honestly thought this was a great plan.

I told more lies over the next few months than I will ever be able to account for. I lied to everybody, including my parents and my children. There was no level too low to stoop for my satisfaction. I slowly pushed every friend, relative, and co-worker that ever gave a damn about me away. The fabulous, new life I so richly deserved turned out to be a job, a hotel room, and a conscience that burned like a raging inferno with guilt. All because that wife of mine was so damned stubborn. *We don't quit* was her motto, and she was determined to live up to it.

On the day I left home, she had taken on a different persona. Gone was the tearful wife and mother who sobbed at the future of her babies. All that was replaced by an air of confidence I had never seen in her. She helped me pack. She hugged me at the door. I didn't return the gesture. She told me she loved me and that we would get through this. I said something eloquent like *yeah, right*.

When I arrived at the hotel, I opened my suitcase. On top of my clothes were the weapons Daphne had chosen to try and crack the armor I was wearing. There were several pictures of our family in happier times. There was a pillowcase she had doused in my favorite perfume of hers and my Bible. I sat and stared at this monument to the life I was trying to kill for about an hour. Then I put the pictures that didn't include Daphne on the dresser, the pillowcase in the top of the closet, and the Bible in the drawer next to the bed. To be honest, I was afraid to touch God's word for fear of it burning my hand. Seeing it reminded me of what a great relationship I once had with Him, not to mention the great people I had abandoned at our church.

Daphne shared with me later that the confidence she displayed was a ruse. I had crushed her, but she wasn't about to let me see it. She wouldn't give me the pleasure of seeing her broken again. For a few months, she spent her nights crying into her pillow and praying I would get smacked in the head by a brick and come to my senses. Her days were filled with taking care of our kids, getting Grayson to his many therapies, and trying to ignore the people who were telling her to let me go. Her dedication to our marriage was awe-inspiring. Even I was impressed, though I tried to act like I thought she was crazy if anyone asked. She wasn't, by the way. I was.

One afternoon, she showed up at the radio station with a proposition for me. She asked me to come home for the weekend. She requested seventy-two hours of alone time with me. She wanted us to put down our swords and try to talk through this mess. *If you still feel the same way Sunday as you do right now, I'll do whatever you want* was her offer. I happily accepted. I figured I could do anything for three days. Then I would tell her nothing had changed, she would get a lawyer, and I would be free. I could finally return to my illustrious life of takeout food, crappy hotel rooms, and the first in what would surely be a long line of girlfriends. I forgot, however, who I was dealing with.

Throughout that weekend, Daphne poured out her heart to me like never before. She didn't plead and beg like I thought she would. She was very matter-of-fact about the life we shared before I stuck my head in my hot pocket. We looked at photo books. She brought out cards I had given her so I could read in my own words just how much I once loved this woman. Saturday night, she broke me. I picked up dinner at our favorite steakhouse and brought it to what used to be home. After dinner, she asked me to join her in the backyard. When I walked out the door, I saw a blanket carefully spread on the ground. She asked me to join her for a few minutes. As we laid there staring at the stars, she opened up even more. She apologized for things she felt she had done wrong in our relationship. She let me know she meant it when she said '*til death do us part*. She had neither the desire or the intention to walk away.

She knew about the affair, but she wasn't angry. She was devastated but not bitter. It didn't seem to ease her pain when I explained it had never gone beyond that exploratory kiss. Yes, there was some level of emotional connection, but it wasn't a leave-one-marry-the-other situation. Then she placed her hand on my chest. In a trembling voice, she looked me in the eyes and said, *That's MY heart. It's MINE.* This would be the only time during the entire weekend she would break down, and it destroyed me. Suddenly the weight of what I was doing came crashing down around me like a brick wall. This was the moment I realized what a total jackass I had become. *We don't quit.* It was time to come home and fix the things I had broken, starting with Daphne's heart.

I would love to tell you this is the happy ending you've been waiting for, but I can't. There were more dumpster fires to light, and before I was finished, I would light them all.

CHAPTER 22

OF ROCKING CHAIRS AND KNEE SURGERY

When you're a stubborn ass with a chip on his shoulder, and you don't like being at fault when stuff hits the fan, marriage counseling is a nightmare. When I broke off my extracurricular social activities to return to my marriage, I wasn't quite as ready as I thought. I begrudgingly agreed to go to counseling with Daphne. I felt I owed her that after all I had put her through. I'm confident our counselor knew within about fifteen seconds that I didn't want to be there. I thought we could handle this at home. Both she and Daphne assured me I was wrong.

And so began the weekly sessions of the blame game. Keep in mind I was entirely in the wrong. Sure, Daphne's insecurity and separation anxiety played a role, but not enough to justify my actions. But I had a brand to protect, and Jerry Broadway didn't do people wrong unless provoked. Therefore, my brain could not accept the fact that what went down was my fault. I bucked and snorted and fought my way through most of our sessions, desperately trying to find a way to paint myself as the victim. The counselor wasn't buying it. It took several months for me to get on board.

I finally began to realize I had allowed myself to be overwhelmed by the stress of my job. Once I allowed stress in, everything else just fell into place. More precisely, everything fell *out of place*. I saw I had become so wrapped up in myself I stopped giving Daphne the time and effort she needed from me. That upset her, causing her to lash out, which caused me to retaliate, and the wheel in the sky started turning. We were trapped in a vicious cycle, and we had finally begun to find our way out when my worst fear came true.

When the Spring ratings for the station were released in August of 2006, I knew I was in trouble. Even though we were still the number one station in the market, our overall ratings share had dropped 3 points. I knew Mr. Cypher had been looking for a reason to get me out of the building. I had been there for thirteen years. I was making, in their eyes, too much money. As soon as he was able to justify my firing by saying the quality of my work had slipped, he pounced. I will be the first to admit my work wasn't the same at that point in my career. I was tired. I felt beaten down. I was on the verge of divorce.

Then there was the little matter of the co-worker I had crushed by going back to Daphne. She thought we were in love. We were not. Somewhere deep down, I thought maybe we could've been eventually, but not now. She worked very closely with Mr. Cypher, and I'm sure she wasn't exactly leading my defense team. Working in the same building with her was torture for both of us. To say I was distracted is an understatement. No wonder the ratings dipped. However, since we were still number one, I thought maybe I would survive. I did not.

I was fired on a Wednesday morning in August. But in true Lou Cypher fashion, he put me on the delayed termination program. To receive my severance package, which contained three months of pay and six months of my precious insurance policy, I would be required to stay in the building and continue working. I was to act as if nothing happened until my replacement was found. Oh, and I had to show him the ropes when he finally arrived. I was expected to do all this with a smile on my face and continue doing the morning show as if nothing had changed. In my mind, I thought *a week, tops. Surely, they have someone lined up already.* Mr. Cypher doesn't work that way.

It was nearly six weeks before the new guy showed up. Six weeks of pretending all was well in my life, knowing I was about to be kicked to the curb with very little chance of finding work in my chosen field in that market. Cypher must have felt good about his final act of skullduggery in my life. He had the ace in the hole, and he played it like a master gambler going all in for the win. I had never hated a man so much. And hate has a way of spilling into other areas of your life. Like your marriage.

Before I knew it, the fighting was back, courtesy of the massive case of red-ass Cypher had given me. Since I couldn't take it out on him for fear of losing my severance, Daphne was elected to be his stand-in. I unloaded on her every time an opportunity presented itself. I was trying to be cool about the job loss thing, but I felt like my heart had been removed from my body.

I loved that job. I *was* that job. What in the world was I going to do without that job? I had never noticed how much I depended on the affirmation that came with that job before. I had let the job become my reason for living. The fact is, I was an attention whore and a bad one. The thought of not having people tell me how awesome I was every day terrified me. I didn't want to be an average person. I didn't know *how* to be normal.

In mid-November, I moved out of the house again. Although it's closer to the truth to say I *got* moved out of the house. New and improved, confident Daphne reached her breaking point, and I came home one day to find everything I owned in a pile under the oak tree in our yard. It turns out even the most dedicated wife on the planet has her limits. I loaded up my truck and went to a friend's house. For the second time in a year, my ego had made me homeless.

One thing I tried to do through this mess was to be somewhat of a dad. I visited the kids as often as I could, and occasionally the five of us would still go out to lunch. It was awkward, but I didn't want the kids to come out of this hating me. Even though people kept telling me kids are resilient and will bounce back from anything, I wasn't so sure. Looking back, it's incredible how many people who should have grabbed me by the collar and told me to get my dumbass home and fix things, instead chose to tell me what they thought I wanted to hear. Yes, kids are resilient, but they are also little human beings, and human beings get emotional scars from trauma. Not one person said that to me. They just kept telling me how strong kids are, and how we don't give them enough credit for being able to deal with divorce.

It was hard to tell at the time, but I was human, too, and human Jerry was a dad who missed his kids terribly. If buying lunch for their mom was the only way to spend a Sunday afternoon with them, then so be it. In the end, it would be one of these awkward lunches that saved my marriage once and for all.

After lunch, I was walking them back to Daphne's car when she realized she had forgotten her purse in the booth. She went back to get it as I was getting the kids buckled into their seats in her car. It seemed like it was taking her an exceptionally long time to get the purse, and when she finally walked out the front door of the restaurant, she was limping. It was clear she was in an incredible amount of pain. She had slipped on some water that was spilled inside. When she went down, she landed on her knee, which was now throbbing and somewhat swollen. I didn't have the heart to leave her in that condition, so we drove the kids to her mother's house, and I took her to the ER to have her knee examined. The swelling had gotten worse, and it was starting to turn various shades of black and purple.

At the hospital, they x-rayed the knee and came back with bad news. When Daphne hit the floor, she split her kneecap down the middle. The x-ray they showed us looked like a cracker that had been snapped in half. There was a perfectly straight break from top to bottom. To make things worse, surgery was the only way to fix it. The recovery would take approximately six weeks, and for the most part, she would be bedridden. The doctor shared that excellent piece of news and then walked out to set up her appointment with the surgeon.

When he left the room, I looked at Daphne, and for just a moment, I saw the face of a frightened, little girl. I could tell her mind was racing. She was contemplating her current situation. For all intents and purposes, she was a single mom with three kids, one of whom had a disability that required constant attention and more than a little traveling for doctor appointments and therapy sessions. Her worthless soon-to-be ex-husband was busy fighting his own demons while living with friends miles away from what used to be their happy home. It took her about four seconds to come to the realization that she was screwed. With tears in her eyes, she looked at me and asked a question that cut to the very center of my soul. *What am I going to do now?*

For the first time in a long time, I genuinely cared about someone other than myself. I knew I had to help, if only for a season. I told her I would move back home and take care of things until she was back on her feet. She didn't really want to bring my drama back into her house, but what choice did she have? She agreed. I took her home, got her settled in, and took the journey to retrieve my belongings.

The surgery was a success, and the recovery time was every bit as bad as we thought it would be. Daphne was in agony, and now two people in the house were getting therapy regularly. She was in an immobilizer post-op, so walking was impossible. Her leg was locked in position and couldn't bend, so sitting wasn't an option. I set her up a pile of pillows that almost looked like the sandbags surrounding a foxhole on the bed and tried to turn the bedroom into a living area. She needed help getting up and down. She needed someone to cook for her. The day-to-day chores of a homemaker had to be taken care of. With the help of my faithful sidekicks, Hayley and Chandler, I managed to keep the place from falling in on itself and take care of her at the same time.

During this process, things changed in my life. I had already found and lost my first job outside of radio and had moved on to my second attempt at a regular occupation selling cars. I sucked at it. I was very frustrated about the level of my suckage and my efforts to survive in a world with no one to perform to. I needed someone to talk to, and since I had systematically chased everyone who ever cared about me away over the past year, the poor lady with the immobilized leg who couldn't get away became my sounding board.

There was only one good thing that came from my brief time as the world's worst car salesman. It was a friendship struck between myself and an older gentleman named Bill. Mr. Bill was a former high school coach with a sweet temperament and a lifetime of wisdom he was more than willing to share if you were interested in listening. We had many long conversations in the parking lot of the dealership during my frequent, prolonged droughts of customers. Something was calming about that man. I could never put my finger on it, but talking to him became the best part of my working days.

His gentle demeanor helped me to find my center again. The funny thing is, I never told him about my troubles at home, and he never asked. We talked about cars and jobs and his relationship with his wife. We talked about hunting, fishing, and sports. We were just two generations of mediocre car salesmen who had found common ground with one another. He was a good thirty years my senior. There was no reason for us to be friends, but for a while there, Mr. Bill was my only friend.

He helped me see the world through his wise eyes. He helped me realize what's really important in life, and it ain't work. Mr. Bill had held many jobs in his life, and he regarded them as just that; jobs. No occupation ever changed him as a man. Bill was Bill whether he was serving in the military, coaching, or trying to sell a farmer a new F150. That was totally foreign to a guy who had become one with his chosen occupation. Bill helped me see the utter stupidity in that.

After a few weeks, Daphne was able to somewhat get up and around. Cabin fever had set in, and she wanted to get out of the house as much as possible. Since going anywhere in a vehicle caused her immense pain, we started going outside in the evenings to sit in a couple of rocking chairs on our front porch. I would set up a box for her to prop her leg on, and we would sit out there and rock like a couple of senior citizens. All the while, I belly-ached about the job and how bad my life was currently sucking. I groaned about how hard it was to find a customer both willing *and* able to buy, and how

I was confident that selling cars was not an endgame for my life.

The funny thing is, all that talking started getting good to me. I remembered how easy Daphne was to talk to, and how her advice was, more often than not, spot on. I remembered how much I enjoyed spending time with her. And then I remembered something that changed my life.

As I mentioned, in the time before I went off the deep end, Daphne and I were very active in our church. One Sunday, when our pastor was out of town, a guest speaker had preached a sermon on marriage. It didn't mean much at the time, because we were happy, but something he said had planted itself in my subconscious as if God knew I was going to need it someday.

The only line I remembered from the entire sermon came roaring into my mind one night after I had gotten Daphne and the kids to bed. I was settling in for another night of back-wrenching tossing and turning on the couch when it came roaring back to me. He was speaking about how married couples fall in and out of love quite a few times during marriage. He had some interesting advice on what to do when you find yourself in that situation. *If you can't love your spouse,* he said, *then ask God to love them through you until you can do it on your own.*

After the *everything you own is under the tree to the left* incident, I had set my sights on yet another woman. I looked at her life and decided I wanted to be a part of it. The grass is always greener, and living with another woman is always happier, right? I did everything I could think to do to get her attention. I said sweet things to her. I did kind things for her. I fell all over myself, trying to make her feel anything at all for me. She wasn't having any, but I still gave it the full-court press. In my mind, being with her would solve all the problems of the world.

Then Daphne broke her knee, I moved back into the house, and all that was put on the back burner until I could get back to it later. I figured I would eventually wear her down, and she, too, would fall victim to my irresistible charms. If you're keeping score, that's two failed attempts at an affair in less than ten months. At that point in my life, to shoot me would have been to waste a perfectly good bullet.

If you can't love your spouse, ask God to love them through you until you can do it on your own. Why was I remembering this now? Was I really thinking about trying to patch things up with Daphne again? I was shocked to discover I was not only thinking about it, part of me wanted it. I realized that since I had come back to take care of her, things seemed different. I had been telling myself, and everyone else, that the only reason I came back at all was to make sure my kids were taken care of. I was starting to realize that, deep down, there may have been an ulterior motive at play. Then I had an epiphany.

What if I asked God to love her through me AND applied the energy and tactics I had been using to gain the eye of another woman to my relationship with Daphne? What if I went back to the roots of our relationship? What if I made Daphne the focus of everything in my life? What would happen if I reverted to my original *charm, baby, charm* technique? Was there a chance in hell she could forgive me for my heinous behavior over the past year? What if I made a list of my biggest fears and admitted that the only reason I had been acting like a total fool was because I was scared to death? What would be on that list?

Jerry's List of Terror and Fear:

1. I am not an adequate husband
2. I am not a sufficient father for Hayley and Chandler
3. I don't have what it takes to be the father of a handicapped kid
4. I don't have the means to take care of Grayson's medical needs
5. I don't know how to survive without radio
6. I'm not smart enough for a career outside of radio
7. I am alone
8. I have no one to turn to
9. I have sinned against God and so many people; I am unforgivable
10. I am not enough

Making that list in my mind crushed what little soul I had left. My God, what had I done? What had I become? Who is this person who looks like me but does the complete opposite of everything I know to be right? I had finally done it. I had found rock bottom. I was living the lyrics to a song by Brad Paisley. *There's two feet of topsoil, a little bit of bedrock, limestone in between. A fossilized dinosaur, a little patch of crude oil, a thousand feet of granite underneath. And then there's me.* I wanted to punch myself in the face. I wanted to run into oncoming traffic and rid the world of my useless presence. I wanted to be me again, but where do I start? I figured the best place would be my knees.

I spent a long time that night confessing my sins. I knew He had seen everything, so there was no need to leave out any of the gory details. I laid it all at God's feet, and I begged for forgiveness. I knew I was the last person on Earth who deserved another shot. Still, if He could take away my guilt and shame, and open the door the tiniest of bits, I would charge through it like a runaway train in an attempt to make things right. Daphne might not give me a third chance, but I was going to ask for it anyway. But I couldn't do it without His help.

The very next night, sitting in those rocking chairs, I hit my knees again. This time, I was in front of Daphne. My Queen. The love of my life. The girl who stole my heart with a thrown piece of ice and a bag of chili dogs. More confessions were made, as I told her the things I had told God the previous night. I told her I didn't expect her to forgive me on the spot. All I wanted was a chance to right the ship. If I had pushed her too far away, I understood. I just needed her to see I was no longer a slave to that voice in my head. I had made my peace with God. Now it was time to do the same with her and the kids. She may not want me as her husband anymore, but I wanted to at least be a part of the family. I wanted to be there for her and the kids. When I was done, I laid my head in her lap and waited for her to say *nice try, jackass*.

She didn't say anything. After a moment of silence that felt like ten hours, she gently ran her fingers through my hair. When I looked up, there were tears on her cheeks. She was stunned by what she had heard. She didn't see any of this coming. She took my face in her hands and said, *Where've you been? I've been looking for you everywhere.*

It would take a few years, some long rocking chair discussions, and more counseling before we would completely put 2006 in the rearview. Thanks to Daphne's unwavering commitment, and God's unconditional forgiveness, we rebuilt our marriage. The wreckage of that year became an even stronger foundation for us, and we have never looked back. *We don't quit.*

In 2007, I launched what would affectionally be known as the Great Apology Tour. I found every person I had slighted, hurt, lied to, or otherwise poorly treated, and personally asked for their pardon. My family was easy. They love me no matter how stupid I may be. Some friends were harder than others. A few were lost forever, and I don't blame them. My real friends, however, forgave and forgot. I went back to church and became a Sunday School teacher. I rejoined the choir. I even gave my testimony at several churches, being as open and honest as possible. At least three couples told me our story inspired them to save their own marriages.

The pause in our happy marriage was a horrible experience when it was happening, but as He will often do, God turned our mess into a blessing. I don't take that for granted. For if I had achieved my goals of divorcing Daphne and starting a new life, I would have missed out on a million blessings that were yet to come. I would have missed a considerable piece of Hayley and

Chandler's childhoods. I would have missed out on the Bud and Broadway Show. I would have missed Grayson showing the world what a miracle truly looks like.

The beach is his happy place...

Hangin' with Keith Urban

Uncle Raymond

Hayley's wedding day

Chicks dig the curls!

Nobody loves you like your Mom...

My Mom with her Grandbabies...

Giving "Dindy" (Cindy) a hug...

Uncle Brandon

Our hero, Dr. Robert Benak...

Miss Kari, G's favorite teacher ever....

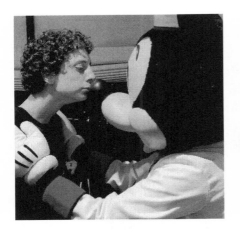

This boy loves his Nee-Nee

Chillin' with Pop

Cousin Zach

Cousin Lexie

Playing Ball with Memaw

Terry Sears, paraprofessional

Billy (my stepdad), Mom and Dad

Mamaw Clark

Brotherly love..

Aunt Amberly

Heather and Kristi, my "sisters"...

The fan club showed up to watch G's pre-game dance...

Gatlinburg with Nona and Pop

Mr. Mitchell Grantham provided the horses that Grayson rode during horseback therapy. A kind man with a soul as gentle as the horses he prvided.

Zac Brown Band

Luke Bryan

American Idol Trent Harmon

Bud Ford, Kelly Rebal, and Jason Aldean

Brad Paisley

Grayson's first and oldest friends are these two. Bentley (the blond) has been in our family for eleven years. Penelope has been with us for five. He loves them like siblings, and they are his playmates, tv buddies, and guardians.

CHAPTER 23

DO'S AND DON'TS

Consider this chapter a public service announcement to all who are currently—or might someday be—friends with a family that is blessed with the responsibility of caring for a special needs kid. These tips are based on seventeen years of experience with friends of all shapes, sizes, colors, and creeds. I'll be the first to tell you that Daphne is an amazing woman, wife, and mom. Having said that, even Wonder Woman has a support system. We have been blessed with some remarkable friends since Grayson came into our lives, and they are a master class in caring. Others dropped the ball at the opening kick-off and disappeared. Here are a few lessons learned from each group:

DO:
*Be there even when we are distracted and don't appear to appreciate you. We do. We are spinning many

plates, and sometimes we get caught up in the whirlwind that is our life. Know this: we see you, and knowing you're there means more than you will ever know.

*Offer your help, if you are so inclined. We are stressed. We are tired. We need some time alone. If you can, offer to keep the kids so we can have a date night, or a weekend getaway, or a nap. Naps are as awesome as they are rare in the early days of learning how to do this.

*Keep us from crawling into a hole. If we've been friends a while, you know us, and you know when we are withdrawing. This life is hard, and sometimes it gets downright depressing. If you see it happening, call us on it. You'd be amazed how much good you can do by showing up with a six-pack or a bottle of wine and just sitting in the backyard with us for a while helping us get centered again.

*Instigate girls/boys night out. We are joined at the hip in our roles as special needs parents, but just like you, we need time apart to relax and regroup. We don't mind watching the kids while you take our partner out for the evening.

*Love our baby. Get down on the floor with him and play. Roll the ball back and forth until you think you're going to pass out from boredom. We will walk through fire for you if you treat him/her with that kind of respect.

*Be there. I know it's already on the list. It's that important.

DON'T:

*Be uncomfortable in the presence of the kid. If you're nervous or just don't know what to say, say THAT. Your awkward silence speaks words to the family that may betray your true intentions. We get it. It's a strange situation. You haven't discovered anything new. It was strange to us at first, too.

*Treat us like we are different. Sure, we may do things differently now, but at our core, we are still the same people we were before, only stronger.

*Tell us what your Great Aunt Sylvia did when her son was born with a disability. Honestly, we don't care. While we are confident Sylvia was a wonderful mother, no two situations are the same.

*Be afraid to touch our child unless we tell you he doesn't like it. We promise it's not contagious. He/she wants and needs your love and affection, just like any other kid. If you can't touch, at least talk to him.

*Pray for God to "fix" our child. He's not broken. God gave him a purpose in life, and his condition is imperative to that purpose, the same as you. Your prayers are appreciated, even coveted, but we don't question the Master Designer around here. To us, he doesn't need fixing. He's perfect as is.

*Make and then break plans regularly because you can't deal with the situation. Sometimes it's a downer, and that may not be for you. That's okay. Just be honest about it. We won't judge. Much.

*Feel sorry for us. We don't want your sympathy. We want your friendship.

*Be wishy-washy. Either be a part of our lives or don't. It's that simple. With everything we have on our plates, we simply don't have the time or inclination to beg you to be our friend. If our new life doesn't fit in with whatever you have going on in yours, we understand that. We don't get to come outside and play as much as we did before, and that's a problem for some folks. Commit to being in or go away. In the long run, you'll be doing us all a favor.

*Tell our son, who can't walk at four years old, that he's just lazy. Even if you're joking. We don't think that's funny, and I know funny.

*Tell us that we can handle this because God never gives us more than we can handle. I've already mentioned it once, but I'll say it again. God never ONCE said that. He gives us more than we can handle all the time so we can learn to lean on Him. If we didn't need God, we wouldn't need God. So put that advice where the sun don't shine.

*Ask stupid questions. A sweet lady in our church once asked me (with a straight face) if we thought we were going to keep Grayson. He was four years old. We had pretty well grown accustomed to having him around by then. I told her yes while chewing off the end of my tongue. It's also bad form to ask what our kid's life expectancy is. Yes, it happened.

*Say stupid things. One summer, we were vacationing in Branson, MO, and we were spending the day at Silver Dollar City. A woman approached Grayson, who was enjoying the day from the comfort of his wheelchair. She commented on how cute he was, then looked at me and said, *I think it's just great that you bring him out in public like this.* I told her (with a straight face) that we try to get him out of the basement at least twice a year so he can get a little sun on his face. Then I quickly pushed him away before I said something I was going to have to pray about later.

*Ask to borrow our handicapped parking placard. It makes you look like an asshat, and nobody likes an asshat.

I've learned through the years that women are better at this than men. However, the men who are good at it are phenomenal. I have a list of men I would take a bullet for based on the love they have shown my family through the years.

CHAPTER 24

DOCTORS ARE NOT IN CHARGE

Having repaired our marriage, Daphne and I continued down the long road of Grayson's treatment. While he was perfectly healthy, his prognosis from early on wasn't great, to say the least. We didn't want to believe the many things we were told he may never be able to do, but we had faith in God, and we certainly believed in our boy. We kept our expectations to a minimum and our optimism at a maximum. We had no clue what he would be able to achieve. We learned early on that he was a fighter, and unlike many of his doctors, we never underestimated him.

If I tried to illustrate every incident of Grayson telling his doubters to kiss his ass without saying a word, this book would be somewhere between *War and Peace* and Stephen King's *The Stand* in length. Nobody has time for that. Some of his achievements are as small as the act of making eye contact when he speaks. Some are much, much bigger.

We begin with talking. We were told almost from the beginning that Grayson's verbal skills would be a mystery until they revealed themselves. With his little brain working at such a delayed state, it was simply impossible to determine what his level of communication ability would be. One doctor thought he might be able to eventually speak a word here and there. Another posed the possibility that he would never utter a coherent syllable. He blew that one out of the water the first time he said Mama, and then Da (Daddy).

Those beautiful words were soon followed by eight straight months of him saying nothing but the word *potato*. He didn't just say it, he made it a constant mantra. He must have genuinely enjoyed saying the word because he put a lot into it. He never said it just once. He said it numerous times, all bunched together in one string. He would take a breath then he would say *tattopotatopotatopotatopotatopotato*. He was also very focused on his work. That's the only word he said for those eight months. Then one day, he stopped, and he never mentioned it again.

I think he was warming up. It was as if he were backstage getting ready to perform, doing a *red leather yellow leather* vocal warmup. And once he was warm, he put that aside and literally created his own language, which my family speaks fluently. The boy never stops talking. Over the years, he picked up or invented words to let us know what he wanted and, more importantly, what he needed.

If you met him, you would have trouble understanding him without a translator, but after a while, you figure it out. These days you can carry on a conversation with him, provided he's not watching Spongebob or Elmo on tv. He regularly scolds me at mealtimes when I don't say grace quick enough. He'll say *Daadeee, Pwayuh.* We don't eat without giving thanks at our house. He makes sure of it!

Once he got the whole talking thing worked out, he moved on to his favorite thing; singing. There is no style of music he doesn't love, and he sings along with almost every song he hears, whether he knows the lyrics or not. Amazingly, he can pick out the tune of a song he hears for the first time, and by the time the second chorus rolls around, he's putting words everywhere they're supposed to be. Some of the lyrics are entirely fabricated in his head, but to him, it works, and to us, it's the most beautiful sound on Earth.

They said he would struggle with dexterity and may never understand simple things, like how to play with toys. Tell that to the people at DirectTV, who thus far have been kind enough to give me several thousand dollars in credit to my account to wipe out charges for movies he consistently rents with the remote control, even though I put a password on it to stop him. He once ordered five films from the On-Demand feature that were in Japanese. I don't mean movies that starred Japanese people. The people in the movie were *speaking* Japanese. I never figured that one out. I tried in vain to find the place on our guide where the Japanese films are kept.

The boy is an evil genius when it comes to electronics. He regularly reprograms phones, iPads, and laptops. He's also quite sneaky, and often picks up our phones when we leave them lying around and makes calls. Our friends and family are so kind to him and always have at least a short conversation with him when he reaches out. There are times we don't even find out he called them for weeks until they bring it up in conversation.

The big one, of course, was walking. From the outset, we were told not to expect much. We were cautioned that if Grayson wasn't walking by his sixth birthday, he would never master that skill. Exactly six days before his sixth birthday, he took his first steps across our living room. It was the most awkward, clumsy walking I had ever seen, and it was magnificent. By the end of that month, he started running and pretty much hasn't stopped since. It's beautiful and terrifying all at once.

In another life, Grayson would have made an excellent Australian. The boy loves to go walkabout. He is an explorer who sees no evil in the world, only things to observe and be amazed by. I'm sure I'm not the first dad to learn that lesson the hard way. Once at Thanksgiving, I was in the backyard overseeing the frying of the turkey while he played in our fenced-in yard.

Unbeknownst to me, someone (probably me) had left the gate open at the end of the house, where he used to go and sit down and watch the world go by. I thought nothing of him being out of sight because he sat at that gate regularly. I was literally reading a book about being a better father when the back door flew open. There stood Daphne, tears running down her face. She asked if I knew where Gray was at the moment. I confidently said, *I sure do. He's over by the gate.* That's when she told me her little sister had picked him up three blocks from the house, trying to open the door of a car parked on the side of the street. He was perfectly safe, thank God. She brought him home, and I spent the rest of that Thanksgiving trying real hard to not be seen.

One of his more memorable adventures happened in a hotel in Hattiesburg, MS, in 2016. I went down the hall to get a drink, and I turned the inside lock on the room door inward so it would block the door open because Daphne was in the shower, and Grayson was watching tv. The vending machines were not far away, so I knew I would only be gone a minute or so. When I got back, Daphne was still in the shower, but Grayson was AWOL. The kid is like a ninja. He waited until I was out of the room, then he followed me. I went left. He went right and found the elevators. Nothing brings him more joy than pushing random buttons, and that's just what he did. Wouldn't you know it? The doors opened up, and away he went.

Moments later, I was in the hallway running up and down, calling his name and having a heart attack. Housekeeping was cleaning a bunch of rooms and had the doors propped open, so I went into each room to look for him. Nothing. I checked the stairs. Nothing. I tried to ask the housekeeping staff if they had seen him. Not one of them spoke English, so now we're playing a bilingual game of charades. After the third *no hablo* I gave up and resumed the search.

Daphne had gotten involved by now, and I'm pretty sure she was just about to murder me with a nail file when we met in front of the elevator. That's when we heard the laugh. It was the unmistakeable devilish chuckle of our little miscreant coming from inside the elevator shaft. Once the terror of losing our child was erased by the peace of knowing we were on his trail, it became funny. I called his name, and he laughed even louder. He was definitely in the elevator. Daphne hit the down button so he would eventually get to our floor, and we'd have him.

Alas, when the doors finally opened, there was no Grayson. Just an empty metal vertical-moving monument to my failure as a parent and a human being. Now I would have to get inside and go to each floor looking for him. It was decided that Daphne would wait on our floor by the elevators, just in case. I was just about to get inside when the second elevator opened, and a lady we had never seen was standing there with Grayson. I guess she could tell by the relief on our faces that she had found the right floor.

Gray had gotten off three levels up, found a random door that looked good to him, and knocked. Thank God this nice lady was in that room and not the modern-day version of Ted Bundy! You learn things as you go when you have kids. That day I learned that anytime I leave a hotel room, I lock him in or take him along. That cuts down on a lot of high blood pressure, along with reducing the amount of stink-eye I get from his mom.

As you can see, Grayson is a problem-solver. He taught us a long time ago that he is always watching and learning. He had seen us use the elevator enough that he figured out how to use it. He didn't know what to do next as far as getting back to us, but for his mind to comprehend mundane things like this is beyond amazing to us. It's the same with ordering movies, calling random people on our phones, and changing the password on someone's iPad. He watches. He sees. He learns. There's a lot of knowledge under his Shirley Temple-level curls; it just takes a while to find a way out.

To further illustrate how his mind comprehends things, I present to you the Xbox. Grayson has been fascinated with video games for most of his life. He watched in his earlier years as I played games with Hayley and Chandler. When he got a little older, he would say *I wan pway,* and we would give him a controller with no batteries so he could push buttons all he wanted while we played. Later we graduated to actually giving him a working controller and letting him drive a race car, or *wace cah,* as he says, for a while.

One day he decided to take matters into his own hands. In a move that fascinates me to this day, he grabbed the controller and turned it upside down and rotated it 180 degrees so that nothing is where it was supposed to be. And he started playing. He has held the controller that way ever since. It's a mystery to me why he does that, but he refuses to hold it the way you or I would.

Somewhere in that beautiful head of his, he made the decision that he could handle it better upside down and backward. I never once tried to correct him on it. Why would I? He could turn it upside down and stand on his head for all I care. Our boy can play video games, and he's really good at driving those *wace cahs.* I'm not about to mess up that formula with something silly like *this is the way everyone else does it.* His problem-solving skills are impressive.

Grayson's life has thus far been a parade of miracles, some small and some massive. One of the greatest, if not THE greatest day of my life, was the day our pastor allowed me to speak to our church for a moment at the end of his sermon. I thanked them for their love and prayers for my family, and especially for the way each of them had wrapped their hearts around Grayson. Daphne was holding his hands as he stood in front of her while I was talking. Then I turned to him and said, *Show them what you can do, buddy.*

He let go of his mom's hands and took the ten or twelve clumsy steps to me. It was the first time anyone outside our family had seen him walk. The air went out of the room for a brief moment as several hundred people gasped at once. Then they erupted in applause as they cheered on my boy and gave praise to God all at once. I sincerely hope that when God calls me home someday, this memory will play in my head one last time before I go.

CHAPTER 25

THE BEST WORST CHRISTMAS EVER

Other than the year of the scorched Earth, our life in Alabama was very Normal Rockwell. We had a modest home, three kids, two dogs, and a cat. Post-radio, I finally found a job I could sink my teeth into in the mortgage industry. I was a loan officer, and I wasn't half bad. We attended church, had a ton of friends, a few extremely close friends, and the best neighbors in town. We were living the American dream. That is, right up until the economy collapsed in late 2008. I suddenly found myself unable to get loans closed. Credit rules tightened. It was getting ugly. I struggled through the best I could, but I had reached the disappointing conclusion that I was about to change professions yet again. Then I got the call.

It seemed a railroad company based out of Florida had put up a rather substantial amount of money to bankroll a friend of the owner who wanted to purchase some radio stations. Said friend then proceeded to run the entire cluster straight into the dirt and found himself, shall we say, financially embarrassed when it came time to pay back the loan. I don't know how much time they gave him, but it eventually ran out, and they took the stations from him to try and get their money back.

They were great railroad men, but they didn't know diddly squat about running radio stations. They were looking for people who knew the business to help them get things rolling. Someone gave them my number. Just like that, in the summer of 2009, I was back where I belonged: inside a radio station.

After several months of rebuilding, I began to assemble my new airstaff with the aid of my Operations Manager, Chris Alan. Chris and I searched near and far to find our team. We put an ad in an industry rag looking for an afternoon host, and four hundred and nine applicants came in. The implosion of the economy had left more than a few folks out of work, and they were so desperate to get back in, even one of the smallest markets in the country looked good to them. I divided the demos with Chris and we got to work listening. We narrowed it down to fifty, then twenty-five, down to ten, and then our final five. One of the five was about to get a new gig and unknown to either of us, was soon to become a significant part of my life. His name was Bud Ford.

Bud was *on the beach*, as we say in the radio industry about someone who's out of work. He was also going to college online to be a meteorologist. He had spent most of his radio career working in much bigger markets. Now he wanted to go to a small area hoping to get on a local television station to hone his skills in front of the green screen. His demo made me laugh. When we called him for the telephone interview, I liked him immediately. During our talk, he shared that he had a little brother who was severely handicapped. With common ground like that, it didn't take long for us to bond.

After we hired Bud, he started on the afternoon shift. I was usually in the building most of the day, and we started going to lunch together fairly often. Many of those meals ended with my stomach muscles hurting from laughing non-stop for an hour. For some reason, when the two of us got together, comedy ensued. We noticed that everywhere we went, people in our vicinity would be laughing right along with us before we were done.

In June of 2010, the decision was made to change out my morning show partner. The station needed a jumpstart. I asked Bud if he would come in and do the show with me for a few days to see what happened. As I write this, I've been trying to figure out what happened for precisely ten years. I've had more than a few morning show partners in my career, and some of them were outstanding, but something different was going on with this one. We seemed to be able to read each other's minds. From the first time we ever opened up the mics, we had a level of trust that can't be explained. I knew without any discussion that if I set up a joke, he would knock it out of the park, and he knew the same about me. That kind of chemistry is rare in our business. It's special. We felt from day one that we were onto something. I knew he would be my co-host inside of ten minutes that first morning.

We did our very best to give Dothan, Alabama, a morning show worthy of a major market, and they rewarded us with ratings that were through the roof. For two years, we were the masters of all we surveyed. Then the railroad dudes sold the damned thing lock, stock and barrel.

The sale didn't come as much of a surprise. We all knew they wanted out from the day they walked in. The surprise came when they told us who they sold the station to. We found out when they called a staff meeting. Into the room walked none other than Mr. Lou Cypher. My heart sank. I knew it was over as soon as his wine-fueled rosy red cheeks rounded the corner.

The firing didn't happen immediately. It was a couple of weeks later when we were told that by the end of the day, we would know whether or not the new owners were going to keep our show. I already knew the answer, but I tried to be a good soldier in hopes they would keep us, and a meteor would crash through the roof and land on top of Cypher's head the next morning. Sadly, neither of those dreams came true.

And so in early December 2011, I was unemployed again. I took it like a man this time. I had learned since the last time this happened that radio was a cool job, but it was just a job. I realized I could survive just fine without it, and while I was crushed that the best show I had ever been a part of was being dismantled, I knew I would be just fine. I didn't even blow a fuse when Mr. Cypher informed us that since his company wasn't picking up our show, and the railroad guys had shut their company completely down, we didn't even qualify for COBRA insurance. I just looked into those evil eyes and smiled. He wasn't going to get to me ever again. As fate would have it, our dance wasn't entirely done.

Once Cypher's company bought our cluster, they were in violation of FCC ownership rules. They controlled too much of the market and were forced to sell off a few stations. They got around this small irritation by forming a new company using the brother of the new owner as the owner of those stations. The FCC rubber-stamped this shady move in about a day-and-a-half. Even though both brothers worked out of the same corporate office in Mississippi, and all the checks came from the same payroll department, they were considered separate entities in the eyes of the government. It's amazing what a man can get brushed under the rug when he's worth thirty million dollars.

For reasons that never made sense outside direct intervention from God, the brother that bought the smaller group of stations decided to make one a Country station. In a move that shocked us all, he promptly hired *The Bud and Broadway Show* back. We would be on a much smaller signal, but we at least had jobs again. More importantly, our show would continue.

We had a few weeks off before the launch of our new station, and I set about the business of enjoying the Christmas season with my family. I was determined this was going to be a great Christmas, and I put a plan in motion to make sure of it.

My kids had never had the opportunity to spend Christmas with my parents, at least not at the same time. Since their divorce, we had shuffled around trying to see them both when we would visit Mississippi, but eventually, traveling for the holidays became too much hassle. Besides, we wanted our kids to be home on Christmas morning. Mom had agreed to spend Christmas with us several months earlier. What she didn't know was that Dad was coming as well. They had long since buried the hatchet and, for many years, had gotten along quite well.

I knew there wouldn't be a problem if they were both there, but if one found out the other was coming, there was a chance they would go squirrely on me and back out. So I kept it to myself. They found out when Dad walked in the door and saw Mom and my stepfather sitting at the diningroom table. I was so proud of what I had done. My whole family was going to be together for Christmas. I was on cloud nine. Forty-eight hours later, it all came crashing down.

It was Christmas morning, and we had just finished exchanging gifts. Dad; myself; my stepfather, Billy; and Daphne's brother, Brandon, had spent the previous evening in the backyard, putting together a trampoline for Grayson. We took him out and let him jump for a while. I made coffee and passed out cups. Then it was off to the kitchen to prepare our traditional Christmas breakfast of pancakes and sausages. I was just beginning to mix the batter when I heard Billy yell my name from the living room. I could tell by his voice that something wasn't right.

I ran into the room and saw my Dad on his knees by the fireplace. I helped him to the couch and tried to find out what was wrong. He had a long history of blood clots, back problems, and high blood pressure. I was trying to narrow down the suspects by asking him questions, but he couldn't seem to get enough air to answer me. Then he started turning an odd shade of gray. I told Daphne to call 911. I suspected he had a heart attack, and I knew we had to move fast.

The paramedics were stationed only a mile away, and they arrived in record time. They put Dad on a stretcher and wheeled him out the back door. My family stood in the living room in a state of shock. Was this really happening? I jumped in the shotgun seat of the ambulance and told them to meet us at the hospital. On the way to the ER, I could hear him in the back. He was in a great deal of pain and was complaining about his back hurting. My heart was pounding, and my mind was on fire. I had never felt so helpless. The world was moving in slow motion around me. Then he got quiet. I told myself they had given him something for the pain, and he was going to be just fine.

They rushed him through the doors of the hospital and immediately got to work. The doctor told me his blood pressure was dangerously low, and his pulse was only reading twenty beats per minute. He told a nurse to take me to another room and bring the family to me when they arrived.

When Daphne arrived, I was still trying to convince myself this would make a funny story when he got well. They brought her to me, and I could feel myself starting to unravel. And then it was over. The doctor came into the room ten minutes later to tell me Dad was gone. They had done all they could, but it appeared he had suffered a pulmonary embolism. He never regained consciousness. I collapsed into Daphne's arms. I don't remember what happened for the next few minutes. They tell me I was inconsolable, and I don't doubt it.

At some point, I asked if I could see him, and they led me to the room where his body lay. Except for the tube they had inserted down his throat to try and help him breathe, he looked like he was taking a nap. His color had returned to normal. I don't know how long we sat there with him, but before we left for home, I asked everyone to leave the room and give me a minute alone with him. I held his hand and told him I couldn't believe he was doing this to me on Christmas, of all days. Then I spent a few minutes looking back over the last two days of his life.

We had spent the entire day together on Saturday doing some last-minute shopping and picking up groceries for lunch on Christmas Day. We attended the Christmas Eve service at our church together. I was so proud to be next to him on that pew. It was the first time we had ever been to church together. Dad came to know Christ later in his life. He spent my childhood sitting on the couch watching Roy Rogers reruns as we left each Sunday morning. But he more than made up for it that Christmas Eve as he participated in the service. He even sang along with the carols. I had never heard him sing before.

Earlier that morning, we gave him a bottle of cologne for a gift. When he opened it, we realized Daphne had picked up the wrong bottle at the store and bought him perfume instead. We laughed hysterically about that because he sprayed it on himself before he knew. I could still smell that perfume as we sat there together in that hospital room. I couldn't help smiling.

I didn't want to leave him, but I knew I needed to get home to the kids. They were probably horrified by what they had witnessed. I kissed him on the forehead, told him I loved him and walked into a strange, new world in which I had no father.

CHAPTER 26

MOVIN' ON UP – PART 2

I went back to work in January of 2012 after getting Dad's funeral behind me, and I went back with a vengeance. Besides Daphne, he was my biggest cheerleader; it was surreal, knowing he wouldn't be there to share my excitement when good things were happening. Losing him so suddenly was a hell of a blow, but it was also the swift kick in the pants I so desperately needed.

Daphne and I had long ago decided we were going to stay in Dothan to raise our kids. We truly loved the small-town vibe, and we wanted them to experience growing up in the country the way both of us did. Through the years, I had been offered, and turned down, several opportunities to leave Alabama for a larger market. I believed I had the skills, but deep down, there was a fair amount of fear of the unknown.

My father taught me many lessons during his time on Earth, but his final lesson may have been the most important one of all. Life is short, and that which is given can be taken away in the blink of an eye. As we made preparations to launch our new station, I vowed that the next opportunity that came my way, I was going to pounce on. As it turned out, I would have to wait nine months to put my money where my mouth is.

The Bud and Broadway Show rocked on as though we had never been off the air. We once again achieved top ratings in the market, and we made more than a little noise while doing it. We were not pleased with the actions of Mr. Cypher, and we made sure he knew we were still around. On the day our station took the number one position in the ratings away from our former station (now owned by Cypher's company), we sent him a massive bouquet of black balloons to express our deepest sympathies for his loss. He was not amused. We didn't care. There was something about our new situation that felt temporary anyway, so we decided to have as much fun as possible while it lasted.

In September, we were called into the office by our general manager. He informed us the company was putting budget cuts into place. Both of us were required to take a pay cut to stay on board. Since neither of us had a bankroll set aside, we took the cut, but we did not take it lightly. We went into my office and made a decision. We both thought we had something unique with our show, but we knew we would never find out if we were right in our current situation. We agreed to start looking for a gig in a larger market. If we were ever going to take our show to the next level, we had to go somewhere we would be noticed.

The first help-wanted ad we responded to was for a start-up station in Tulsa, Oklahoma. We sent in our demo on a Tuesday morning. Wednesday afternoon, I was on the phone with the program director setting up a trip to Oklahoma for an interview. A week later, we were offered the job. All that was left to do now was convince my kids this was going to be awesome. Daphne was with me every step of the way, but Hayley had just graduated high school, and Chandler was in his junior year. It wasn't fair, and I knew it, but neither was being homeless. They reluctantly agreed, and we were off. After nineteen years in Dothan, we were pulling up stakes and moving from a small to a medium-sized market. It was time to fish or cut bait. Sink or swim. Poop or get off the pot.

Our first (and probably last) music video

Picking up our CMA Awards

CHAPTER 27

A STAR IS BORN

When you start a new morning show in a market where absolutely no one knows who you are, one of your first missions is to reveal the "character" of everyone on the show. Bud and I knew the only way to successfully let our audience get to know us was to be blatantly honest. In our business, the listener is often regarded as a mindless robot going about their lives, paying no attention to what we say, and their intelligence is regularly called into question. We don't share that opinion. We believe people are busy, to be sure. Too busy, in fact, to put up with BS in whatever quantity it's being served. If someone has chosen to make you a part of their insanely busy morning, the least you can do is be honest about who you are. Nobody likes a fake friend, right?

From the day Grayson was born, I always talked about him on my show, same as with Hayley and Chandler. The people in Alabama knew everything there was to know about the older kids in my house. They knew about Grayson as well, but there weren't many stories I could tell about him during those years because of his condition and the fact that he was so developmentally delayed, so he didn't do a lot.

That all changed when we moved to Tulsa. Grayson was starting to assert himself into our daily lives with a personality that overshadowed any issues he had. He had always been super cute, but now that he could get up and around, and to some degree, communicate, he was becoming quite the comedian. Since Hayley and Chandler were practically grown and out of the cute kid doing cute things stage, I decided to bring Grayson front and center and start sharing his many adventures on the air.

After a few stories, I started posting more photos on social media. Once people heard about him, they were intrigued; when they saw his undeniable cuteness in living color, they were hooked. It occurred to me one night while I was reading through dozens of comments from folks who wanted me to know how Grayson had made them smile and made a bad day better that there was something at work here. I had long held the belief that God had given Grayson a purpose in life, just as He had given one to each of us. I realized at that moment that Gray's mission is entangled with my own. I believe in my heart that I am doing the job God put me here to do.

As an entertainer, I have a unique platform to show the world that you can be a Christian with a healthy relationship with God and still enjoy life. You don't have to be a self-righteous stick-in-the-mud that sits in judgment over the world to be a Christian. That's religion, not Christianity. There is a vast difference between the two, and I've spent my entire career trying to make that point. Now I was starting to understand Grayson's purpose. It is simple. His purpose is to bring joy to all he meets, and he is a master at his craft. I realized that by combining my platform with his story (and those curls that melt everyone's heart). Together we could show the world that kids like Grayson should be celebrated and adored by the world, not shunned and misunderstood.

Every story I told—be it the fact he is the worst hide-and-seek player *ever* because he runs into the walk-in closet, closes the door and then starts yelling *where's Grayson* in his broken language, or the time we bought him an electric ride-on 4-wheeler for Christmas and forgot to show him how to stop it once it started, which led to a nine-mile-per-hour chase through the streets of our neighborhood—made Tulsa fall in love with him a little more. I was creating a monster, but it was the coolest monster ever conceived.

When it was appropriate to do so, Daphne would bring Grayson to station events. He loved to get out and look at the lights of the State Fair or talk to anyone who would stop at a festival. The boy got more visitors than Bud and Broadway, and he was loving every minute of it. The thing I loved most was seeing the smiles on the faces of every single person that stopped to say hi to my little dude. I know this sounds like a dad bragging about his kid, but it ain't bragging if you can back it up, and I can back this up. It is impossible to be in the presence of Grayson Broadway without smiling. That's his superpower.

I don't have any data to back this up, but I genuinely believe Grayson has changed more than a few lives. His purpose is being achieved every day. It's not just parents of other special needs kids that come to see him when we're out. It's parents and other kids who may have never been in contact with someone like him. People who may have been afraid to approach a child who isn't like other children have learned that it's more than okay to stop and interact with him. And if they can do it with him, they can do it with the next special person they meet. Watching these interactions makes my entire family so proud and happy. We will never have to worry about Grayson being shunned. Our prayer as a family is that the lessons he teaches every day will have the same effect on others.

Tulsa, Oklahoma, is a beautiful place, and the people there were very good to the Bud and Broadway team, and to my family. We moved our show there with a mission if you remember. We needed to be somewhere that would get the attention of the major players in our business. We wanted to be in a major market. We wanted to see whether we could play with the big boys. Three years after moving, we got the attention we wanted. Things were about to change yet again. Not just for Bud and Broadway, but for the Broadway family. Especially the little curly-headed miracle boy. He was famous in Dothan. He was a big hit in Tulsa. Little did any of us know, he was about to become a full-fledged rock star.

CHAPTER 28

MOVIN' ON UP – PART 3

February 28, 2016 was the day all our dreams came true. We moved our show to St. Louis, market number 22. We were in the big leagues. We were a major market morning show. We set up shop and got right to work doing all we could to dominate the market. To date, our show has been blessed with two Country Music Association Awards nominations, including a win for Major Market Personality of The Year in 2018, and two Academy of Country Music Awards nominations, including a win for Major Market Personality of The Year in 2018. We were named Best Morning Show by the Missouri Association of Broadcasters in 2019, and have been named Best Local Morning Show in St. Louis for three consecutive years by the readers of St. Louis Magazine. It hasn't sucked at all, and we couldn't be more humbled or grateful for the experience.

In the course of our years here in The Lou, Grayson became an even more significant part of our show. The older he gets, the better the stories get, because the boy is a non-stop whirlwind of exploration. By that, I mean he's into *everything.* He's also fully developed a personality now, and he's quite funny. Occasionally someone will chastise me for commenting on or "making fun" of things he does that make me laugh. When that happens, I'm fond of quoting that great American orator, Bobcat Goldthwait.

Bud and I opened a stand-up comedy show for Bobcat a few years ago. During that show, he told a story about being on an airplane with the American Special Olympics Team. It was a heartwarming story, but it was also quite funny. Bobcat told the crowd he didn't want to hear any complaints because the people on that plane were entertaining and to deny them that is to deny them their humanity, and that's not fair. That's my response. I can't say it any better than that. Grayson is funny, and he knows it. Sometimes he does things just to get a laugh. You will never convince me otherwise.

St. Louis is a city swamped with concerts. Being in the center of the country has its advantages in that department, and we regularly host between forty and fifty shows a year, and that's just the Country acts. I wouldn't even hazard a guess at the total number of shows that happen here annually. Many of the Country concerts are held at the Hollywood Casino Amphitheatre. New Country 92.3, our station, has a massive presence at these shows, and you will more often than not find Bud and Broadway at our display, working the crowd like carnival barkers before the shows.

Daphne frequently brings Grayson to these concerts, because music is the great love of his life. It is here that his fan club gathers. As soon as word gets out that he is on-site, people come from all over the grounds to say hi. Some get pictures with him. He eats up the attention the same way he eats Peanut M&Ms, his favorite snack. He can't get enough of those either.

I didn't realize just how big a star the boy is until one Friday night when Daphne had to go out of town for some family business. Grayson stayed behind with me, and I took him to work with me at the amphitheater. Since I was on duty, I asked Scott, our program director at the time, if his husband Mel would mind pushing Gray around in his wheelchair until I was done. Grayson loved Mel, and the feeling was mutual. I knew he was in good hands.

They took off on a stroll around the grounds for about an hour. When they came back, Mel informed me my son was more famous than we knew. Keep in mind, Grayson doesn't wear a sign that says *I'm Broadway's kid Grayson* when he's out in public. Mel said he couldn't push the wheelchair more than ten or fifteen feet at a time, because people kept stopping him to ask whether it was Grayson he was pushing around. He was astounded at how many people knew him just by seeing him. Thank you, social media, for giving him that notoriety.

I suppose before we're done with this crazy ride, I'll have to sign him with my agent. I'm being facetious, but who knows what the future holds for him? We don't draw any lines, because we don't want to box him in. That's been a running theme his entire life, and we're not about to change it now. I'm just thankful I've been able to see it unfold.

In June of 2017, just a year after arriving in Missouri, Grayson's older brother Chandler decided to move back to Alabama on his twenty-first birthday. He didn't like being a midwesterner. He wanted to go back South. He wanted to be on his own, spread his wings, yadda yadda yadda. The fact is, he was chasing a girl, and she wouldn't come to him, so he went to her.

Daphne was devastated. I was happy we were lowering the testosterone levels in our house by half. There can only be one rooster in the henhouse, and Chan had decided he was rooster material. I knew exactly how it was going to end, but he wanted to be a man. I took him aside the day before he left and told him that this was, bar none, the stupidest thing he had ever done in his life, but I truly admired him for having the guts to do it. It was a big, man-sized move.

We were all a little concerned about how Grayson would handle the change in the house. He was accustomed to *Can-muh* being around all the time. They were the best of friends, and we knew this was going to be a considerable test for Gray. It only took a few days for me to realize he was going to be okay. The gaping hole left behind by Chandler's departure was quickly filled by big sister Hayley.

From the very beginning of Grayson's life, Hayley has been so much more than a sister. She is his second mother. She protects him with the fierceness of a wild animal. She has doted on him since day one, and she wasn't about to let him feel like he was missing anything when Chandler left the nest.

I don't know how to express my gratitude for Hayley. For seventeen years, she lightened her mother's load by always lending a hand, whether we asked her to or not. She took him for walks to give us breaks. She took him to parks just because. She always introduced her friends to him, and soon they, too, would fall in love. She went to doctor's appointments, therapy sessions, and meetings at the school with us. She didn't want to miss anything that had to do with his education or treatment. For years, she has insisted Gray sits on her side of the table when we go out to eat because she wants to help feed him. She's amazing. I've never seen a brother and sister with this kind of bond. It's a great comfort to Daphne and me to know that if something were to happen to both of us, Grayson would be in great hands.

She got married in the Fall of 2019, and we were once again faced with Grayson having to adapt to a huge shift in his daily life. Fortunately, Chandler had decided he wasn't quite as ready to be out of the nest as he initially thought. After being out of the house for just a shade over three years, he came back home. I never said I told you so, by the way. I didn't have to. He told me I was right about everything. It was one of my better father moments. Having him back home took some of the sting out of Hayley being gone.

Before she married her Prince Charming, Seth, she made sure he had plenty of exposure to Grayson. When he came to me to ask permission to marry her, I made sure he understood what he was getting into. Someday Daphne and I will no longer be able to take care of Grayson, and Hayley long ago agreed that when that time comes, he will move in with her. To his credit, Seth told me he was willing and ready to take on that responsibility when the time came. I figured he was blowing wind up my skirt to get my blessing, but went along with it because I knew how much Hayley loved him. He changed my mind during their wedding. They wrote their own vows. He included in his promises that when the time came, he would love Grayson and welcome him into their home. I had to pick my feet up off the floor to keep them out of the puddle of all the hearts that melted around me. They were sold, and so was I. Daphne and I sleep a little better knowing that even when our ability to be there for Grayson wears thin, there's a backup plan.

Because of the years she has spent with Grayson, Hayley chose to be an occupational therapist. Her dream is to work with and help kids like her baby brother. As her parents, there is simply no way we could be more proud.

CHAPTER 29

LIFE WITH THE G-MAN

The list of things Grayson has brought into or enhanced in our lives is endless. It includes things like hope, understanding, patience, determination, and love. For me, the word that means the most is happiness. I've never encountered a soul filled with so much joy. I would give anything to see the world as he sees it for just one day. The picture on the cover of this book is my favorite shot of Grayson. Daphne took the photo when he was very young. Thousands of times, I have looked at the picture, marveling at the wonder on his face as he stares at that dandelion. I've made it a life goal to try and look at mundane things in my life with that same wonder and appreciation.

Grayson fills our days with laughter. Sure, he has bad days like everyone else. Still, even the worst day for him can be fixed with a glass of chocolate milk and an episode of Spongebob Squarepants. We spend hours watching that show. We've seen every episode dozens of times. When he locks in on something, he's loyal to a fault. With all the options in the world of television, there are six shows that he watches consistently; *Spongebob*, *Sesame Street*, *Blues Clues*, *Barney and Friends*, *The Voice*, and *Ellen*. There's a common thread among these shows. That thread is music. There's nothing he loves more.

I don't know when he got hooked on *Ellen*, but when he's tired of cartoons and puppets, he'll bring me the remote and say, *Wah Ehwen*. If I don't change it fast enough, he turns on the pitiful and says *Pwee Daddy Pwee Wah Ehwen*. Even if I wanted to, I couldn't say no to that. When he wants non-stop music, we have several years of CMA and ACM Awards shows saved on the DVR. I mean, sure, they are the episodes in which Bud and Broadway won awards, but that's beside the point. When he wants that, he asks for *Kee Uh-Bun* (aka Keith Urban).

To give you a glimpse of life with Gray, here are a couple of my favorite stories:

From early on, when he started speaking, when we were out riding in the car, he would always get excited when we got back into our neighborhood, or anytime he realized we were slowing down to turn into a driveway or a parking lot. He would say *Hey geh wha?* (hey, guess what?) One of us would dutifully say, *What?* And he would say *we home*. It didn't matter back then if we were actually home, or going to the grocery store when we turned, he would announce that *we home.*

At least once every year, we go back to Mississippi to stay with Uncle Ronnie and Aunt Darla on what we refer to as the family farm. On one trip, Daphne had gone shopping with Aunt Darla, Kristi, and Heather, and left Grayson with myself and Uncle Ronnie. It was late in the day, and we were getting ready to put a chicken in the air fryer for dinner. We got it all set up, and I set the timer on my phone. That's when Grayson announced he was *weddy go wide* (ready to go ride). Riding Uncle Ronnie's side-by-side has always been one of Grayson's favorite things on Earth. When we go home, there are times when he will disappear. We don't worry about him at all because we know exactly where to find him. One hundred percent of the time, he will be in the yard sitting in the shotgun seat of the side-by-side. When he sees you, he will say *key key*, which is his way of saying *get the key and take me for a ride.*

This particular trip, the side-by-side was not working. Fortunately, Kristi had recently purchased a golf cart, so that would be our means of travel for the day. What I didn't realize was that other people had been riding the cart all day long, and the batteries were just about toast. I loaded the boy up and away we went down the backroads of Soso, Mississippi. After we had been riding about ten minutes, I heard the sad sound of the batteries going zcheeeewwwwww as they died a slow, painful death.

This presented a serious problem because we were half a mile from home with a dead battery, and we were stuck at the bottom of a hill. I reached for my phone to call Uncle Ronnie for a lift. That's when I remembered the chicken in the air fryer, and the timer I had set. I left the phone with him so he wouldn't miss the timer. I had no way of calling for assistance. There was no chance I was going to ask Grayson to walk that far. Our choices were to wait for someone to come by, or I could try to push the golf cart home. We could have waited two or three days without seeing another vehicle on that road, so I decided to put my back into it and get him home.

In case you don't know, pushing a golf cart up a hill is a miserable experience. I was giving it everything I had. I was drenched in sweat, and my back was on fire by the time we reached the top. I thought we would then be able to give it one more push and coast down the backside of the hill from hell, which would put us almost at the driveway to the farm. We coasted roughly nine feet before it stopped. And this time, it was done.

So I explained to Gray we were going to have to hoof it for a bit. We were close enough now that I could carry him if his little legs gave out. He did great with our impromptu cardio session. When we got to the end of the driveway, we got ready to turn and walk up to the house, Grayson tugged at my shirt and said, *hey geh wha?* I knew what was coming, so I said *what?* He looked me dead in the eye and said, *walk.* I gave the little smartass a hug and told him that's exactly right. The kid's timing is professional grade.

The best stuff with Gray always seems to happen when there's nobody around but the two of us. Hayley's middle name is Morgan. Through the years, he had heard us call her Hayley Morgan when she was in trouble, or when we really needed her. He picked up on that somewhere down the line, and to this day, when he gets frustrated with her about something, he will very sternly call her *Hayley Mo-Gan*. I never understood why he didn't do that to Chandler because God knows he heard us say Jacob Chandler many more times than he heard Hayley Morgan. You know, because teenage boys.

One afternoon we were alone at home, and I was installing an electrical outlet in our bar, which I had just rebuilt. I was having a bit of trouble running the wires through the floor from the basement, and I was getting a bit frazzled. That's when Grayson came down the stairs and said *I want a nack* (I want a snack). I explained to him I was busy, and I would get him a snack as soon as I finished my work. He went back to his room but was back again about two minutes later. *Daddy, I want nack cookie*, he said, cuteness dripping off every word. Once again, I tried to tell him he would have to wait. I could tell he wasn't happy about it, but he went back to his room.

I didn't realize that we were in a def-con 5 emergency snack situation. Less than a minute later, Grayson was back on the stairs. This time, the cuteness had been replaced by pure attitude when he said *Daddy, I want nack cookie NOW!* By now, I had reached the stage of stress over those stupid wires that sweat was forming on my forehead as if I had just eaten a whole ghost pepper. It was getting close to throwing a wrench across the room time. I was much more matter-of-fact about it this time when I told him he could not have a cookie right now and he needed to get back in his room and watch tv. That's when he stomped his foot and said *I want nack cookie now, DADDY MORGAN!*

As I put the Oreos in his bowl, I apologized to him for taking so long. I was afraid for a minute there he was going to send *me* to my room.

Earlier this summer we were visiting family in Alabama. Grayson and I were at my Mother-in-law's house while she was doing some shopping with Daphne (properly masked and socially distanced, of course). There was a knock on the door and when I opened it, I saw Daphne's brother, Brandon, on the porch. I stepped outside to talk to him for a minute so as not to interrupt Grayson, who was spending some quality time in *Elmo's World*. Ten minutes or so went by, and I decided to peek inside to make sure he was all good. When I opened the door, I heard him say very loudly, *Fwench fwies, and ummmm....*

I jokingly said, *French fries? Are you ordering lunch?* That's when I heard a woman very sweetly say *honey, is there a grown up there I can talk to?* I realized I had broken a major Grayson rule, and left my phone inside where he could see it when I walked outside. I grabbed the phone to see who he had been talking to about the current potato emergency we were evidently experiencing. The sweet voice on the phone belonged to the local 9-1-1 operator. He had called them to put in a lunch order. It turns out they don't deliver.

If you think it's a struggle trying to get your politically charged friends and family to put a mask on in public during a pandemic, find yourself a kid with Autism who hates to have anything touching him above the shoulders. I've never wrestled a bear, but I'm pretty sure I would have better luck getting a full-grown grizzly into a figure-four leglock than I've had getting Grayson to wear his mask. Needless to say, we don't go out much in the world of Covid-19.

CHAPTER 30

OH, THE PLACES YOU'LL GO!

Daphne and I have been asked a few times over the years if we would go back and change things for Grayson if we could. That is an odd question, albeit an interesting one. Would we go back if possible and transform him into a "normal" kid? Would we want him to have a life that mirrors the lives of other kids his age, with girlfriends and teen angst and friends that hang out on the weekend? As tempting as it may be, I have to say no. I don't know if *typical* Grayson would have had the effect on his fellow man that *special needs* Grayson has had and continues to have. I still believe God made Grayson precisely the way He wanted Grayson to be to further His kingdom. If you think that's silly, okay. Write your own book. I see God at work every day in Grayson's life.

Watching the world through Grayson's innocent eyes has been the joy of my life. It is a true pleasure to witness his wonder in everything from bubble wrap to automatic hand dryers. He is always amazed, always curious, and always, ALWAYS full of joy. That's just a few of the great things about living with a kid with special needs.

As I've watched Gray through the years, I have often found myself wondering if HE is the typical one, and the rest of us are actually the handicapped ones. To put it in a Biblical perspective, we were created to love our fellow man unconditionally. Not just our immediate family members and close friends, EVERYBODY. It takes all of twelve seconds watching the news or reading the Internet to realize we royally buggered that concept. Hate, bigotry, and bias seem to be the rule of the day for the general population.

I believe Grayson's greatest gift to the world is that there is absolutely no trace of hate, bigotry, or bias to be found in him. He is the picture of innocent love. Black, white, yellow, red, and brown are nothing more than words to him. When he looks at a person, that's what he sees; a person. And when he sees a person, he gives them unconditional love.

In 2013, we gave him that electric 4-wheeler I mentioned earlier in hopes that he would finally get over his fear of riding in or on a vehicle other than our car. Up until that point, he was terrified of anything that rolled. He got over it fairly quickly. Every afternoon for two years, you would find one or all of us in the front yard, so Grayson *go wide*. Our neighborhood was full of kids back then, and they would all come out to play about the same time as Gray every afternoon. Without fail, every time he would get close to one of them, he would stop the 4-wheeler, get off and say *go wide?* Because he wanted to share his fun with them. Some would take him up on the offer, others would politely decline and he would get right back to riding.

I see his interactions with others, be they children or adults, and I again wonder who is handicapped here? Gray doesn't judge on appearance, race, wealth, religion, sex, education, favorite football team, or any of a million reasons we regular folks use in our mind to determine whether someone is worthy of our time and attention. The boy just flat-out loves everybody, with zero strings attached. I've come to the conclusion that this world would be a lot better off if the rest of us took on some of the characteristics of the "disabled," "special needs," "handicapped" people in our midst. I try, but in all honesty, I'm not as good at it as Gray.

Seventeen years ago, Daphne and I were blessed by being charged with teaching our little guy the things he needed to know so he could get by in the world later in life. Over those years, it has become painfully evident that the teacher in this family is Grayson. The things he teaches us with each passing day make it easier for *us* to get by.

And so we celebrate seventeen years of miracles. Seventeen years of doctors, therapists, teachers, and friends who have all been touched by our miracle. Seventeen years of holding on while letting go. Seventeen years of total amazement, witnessing his unwavering determination and endless love for everyone in his path. Seventeen years of moments that terrified Daphne and me; moments he waltzed through like they were nothing.

He will graduate high school as a member of the class of 2022. I know without a doubt that class will bring significant changes to our world. I also know without question that God has big plans in store for a young man who was given a grim prognosis at first, so he lived. Who wasn't supposed to walk, so he ran. Who wasn't supposed to speak, so he sings. Who wasn't supposed to be able to interact socially, so he made the world fall in love with him.

Put a wall in front of him, and Grayson will find a door. Or a window. Or a way around. He doesn't know how to quit. He gets that from his mom. He literally doesn't know what failure means, much less how to do it.

The Broadways are not the same people we were that night when everyone sat in our living room in stunned silence, wondering what was next. How could we be? We have stared into the abyss, and we have seen the void completely disappear, awash in the light of miracles.

EPILOGUE

In December of 2019, we found ourselves at a beautiful place called Give Kids The World in Orlando, Florida. We were there because an organization known as The Dream Factory had presented our family with an all-expenses-paid week at Disney World. The Dream Factory operates much like Make-A-Wish, but they focus on non-terminal kids like Grayson. If you think that sounds wonderful and you'd like to help them, you already have. A portion of the proceeds from this book will be donated to them. I want every kid like Grayson to experience what he did during that week.

Between visits to the parks and hanging with Mickey, Daphne and I found ourselves sitting on a park bench inside the *Give Kids The World* campus, which is almost a theme park itself. We were soaking up the Florida sun while enjoying an ice cream cone. Hayley, Seth, and Chandler had taken Grayson to the playground, and we took the opportunity to sit down and relax for a minute.

While we were sitting there, another family approached us with a cute, little red-headed boy. He was suffering from some unknown illness (*Make-A-Wish* also sends kids to GKTW). He looked to be about four years old, and he was intrigued because I was feeding pieces of my ice cream cone to a squirrel that was no stranger to being fed ice cream cones. The squirrel was inches away from my hand, eating, and this little dude was hypnotized. We talked to them for a couple of minutes, and they walked away, enjoying a brief respite from whatever challenge they were facing.

Looking at the girl of my dreams in that beautiful Florida sunshine, I reminded her that not too long ago, that was us. She knew exactly what I meant. So many unanswered questions. So much uncertainty. We began to reminisce about our time with Grayson. We talked about how lucky we have been to have support from so many friends and family members, but most of all, Hayley and Chandler. We were so grateful they were allowed to join us on the trip.

In a moment that could only be shared by parents in our situation, I asked her if she ever wished things had turned out differently for Gray. With a wisdom that defies logic and more love than I will ever deserve in my life, she looked at me with those gorgeous eyes and said *of course not. If things had been different, we wouldn't be eating ice cream in Florida right now.*

I smiled because I knew where she was going. There's no point in even thinking about things being different. Our lives are exactly as they are meant to be.

About The Author

Jerry Broadway is a 30 year veteran of the Country Music radio business. He has won numerous accolades for his work, including a Country Music Association Award and an Academy of Country Music award for Personality of The Year. He also picked up a plaque for coming in 5th place in the 6th grade spelling bee which his Mother proudly displayed on her living room wall until the day she died. Jerry is the proud Father of three great children; Hayley, Chandler, and Grayson. He has been married to the love of his life for 27 years (25 of which have been wonderful). He is currently the co-host of the nationally syndicated Bud And Broadway show and lives in St. Louis, Missouri, where he sits on his deck in the evenings drinking Captain and Coke, dreaming of retiring to Jamaica someday. This is his first book, but he has composed several dozen bad songs, some fairly decent love letters, and fifteen years worth of well thought out Facebook posts that go largely ignored by all but his closest friends and family.....

Post Credits Scene

Since I completed this project, a rather significant change has occurred in our lives. On May 1ˢᵗ, 2020, the Bud And Broadway Show was let go from our dream job due to COVID-19 related budget cuts in our former company. At the time of this writing, the ink is barely dry on a new contract we just signed to syndicate our show nationally. Moving on up, part 4! God has delivered once again, and we are beyond excited to see what's down the road for the Bud and Broadway show.

In the interim, it occurred to me that I left out some important information in the context of this book. I mentioned in an earlier chapter that the people who work in radio have a wicked sense of humor, and boundaries don't really exist. I brought that up because I knew what I was going to be dealing with when I went back to work after having my testicle removed. What I failed to share with you was some of the more colorful jokes that were made at my expense. So here are a few of my favorites:

1. What's Jerry's favorite brand of ink pen? Uni-Ball
2. What's Jerry's favorite card game? Uno
3. What song always makes Jerry cry? One Is The Loneliest Number
4. Who is Jerry's favorite country singer? Lefty Frizzell
5. Co-worker and current TV star Mitch English (Upon handing me a Mounds candy bar) I want you to have this, because sometimes you feel like a nut, and sometimes you don't....

And finally, this one from my dear friend and former morning show partner, Tom Nebel:

6. Jerry's greatest regret is that he has but one nut left to give to his country.

Thank you for finishing the book. You'll never know what that means to me. May God bless you in everything you do.

Acknowledgments

Writing a book is hard. Like, stupid hard. It's also a team effort. The words are mine, but so many have contributed to my life, and therefore this book, that it would be impossible to thank them all. I am, however, going to make a run at it. Heartfelt thanks to the following:

Daphne Broadway, thank you for the patience, the understanding, the love, and the occasional rum and coke.

Hayley and Chandler, you guys are amazing. I could write another book on nothing more than how proud I am of both of you.

The Davis family, including Teresa Herold , Micheal Harrison, Brandon Harrison, Amberly Money , Nikki Bush, Paige Bush Scruggs , Chris Davis, Danielle Davis, Eric Davis, and Zach West. Thank you for giving me my partner in crime, and for all your ontributions that made her the unbelievable person she is today.

Raymond and Stephanie Walters. You are so much more than sister and brother-in-law to us. Thank you.

Lexie Robinson. Grayson is lucky to have you in his life. Thanks for loving him so well.

Glenda Gandy, Wanda White, Brenda Stringer, Donnie Ishee, Ricky Broadway, Tammy, Steve Broadway, Wayne Broadway, Stacey Holifield, Jamie Rhodes, and Wayne Rhodes. My cousins. My peeps. My original posse. Those who have had my back since childhood.

Brenda Stringer. Thanks for taking the time to teach your little pain- in- the- neck cousin to read. You opened up the world for me, instilling a love for books and an eventual desire to write. Basically, this is all your fault.

Luke Stevens, Jason Bradford, Mac Davis, Tim Gay, Brad Harris, Mark Givens, Mr. Ralph Givens, Bill Knowles Matt Singletary, Jim Ethridge, Dewayne Barr, Cecil Sanders and the men at First Baptist Church Headland, AL. I learned how to be brutally honest from you.

Sam and Eddie Farham. I don't even know where to start. You have never once failed to make me smile, even when times were at their worst. You may know this already, but Daphne and I love you dearly.

Pat and Roddy Cook. Thank you for making us feel like we have been a part of your family since the day we met.

Cindy Smith, Gina Bradford, Judy Dykes, Amanda Deschaine, Connie Hartzog, and Laura Ethridge. Thank you for being there when Daphne needed you the most.

Kari Kenyon, Cheryl Luce, Mike Larson, Terry Sears, Brooke Jones, Erin Bell, Kara Dykes, Susan Howze, and Mitchel Grantham. Just a few of Grayson's teachers, therapists, and paraprofessionals that have done so much to help him through the years.

Dr. Robert Benak.

Bud Ford, Tom Wall, and Becca Walls. You three are the team I was born to be a part of, and I thank God every day for the four hours of non-stop laughs and fun we loosely refer to as our job.

Carson James. Thanks for teaching me how to do radio right. Without you there is no career for me. Period.

Amy Hibbs. Thank you for the friendship and the prayers.

Ken Stokes. Thanks for making me laugh until I hurt every single time we talk.

Ron and Kim Graves. John and Kathleen Fricke Tony and Cindy Burgess, Tom and Lori Kehoe, Sean and Julie McIntosh, Jason Spencer, Steve and Kathy Levers, Traci and Jeff Fuchs, Chris and Keri Kenyon, Karen and Barb Behlmann. Thanks for showing us that new friends can feel like old friends.

Our neighbors, past and present. Thanks for your kindness and understanding towards Gray, and thanks for catching my little runaway from time to time.

Ronnie and Darla Clark. Thank you for stepping up when I needed you most, and for making my family a part of yours.

Grayson. You have changed me on a cellular level, Little Man. Thank you for giving me purpose, and for teaching me the importance of celebrating tiny little things that others take for granted.

Made in the USA
Coppell, TX
05 November 2020